Instructor's Manual

to accompany

Carter/Gradin

Writing as Reflective Action
A Reader

Duncan Carter
Portland State University

Sherrie Gradin
Ohio University

Longman

New York Boston San Francisco
London Toronto Sydney Tokyo Singapore Madrid
Mexico City Munich Paris Cape Town Hong Kong Montreal

Instructor's Manual to accompany Carter/Gradin, *Writing as Reflective Action: A Reader*

ISBN: 0-321-07847-0

1 2 3 4 5 6 7 8 9 10- VG -03 02 01 00

Contents

Introduction

As we suggest in the Preface, at the heart of *Writing As Reflective Action* is a belief in reflection and reflexivity as crucial to learning, and thus to thinking and writing. We think that students should be able to communicate well already assimilated knowledge in the typical thesis-driven text. However, and this is an important however, we also feel strongly that students should use writing as exploration, as a mode of reflexivity. This means that some of their writing may be more exploratory or essayistic in form, more tentative, and too complex to fit a thesis-driven format. (We urge you to read Donna Qualley's theoretical work, *Turns of Thought: Teaching Composition As Reflexive Inquiry*, as a way of understanding more fully what we mean by reflexive and essayistic writing. We find her book an invaluable companion to ours. Likewise, Gradin's *Romancing Rhetorics: Social Expressivist Perspectives on the Teaching of Writing* will help contextualize the practice we work with here.)

Since we want students to be able to do both kinds of writing, we have structured the text in particular ways. For example, some formal writing prompts clearly call for students to take what they currently see as "known" knowledge and to write a persuasive paper, a thesis-driven paper, a paper sure of its answers. Other formal writing prompts, however, call for more reflexivity in the writing, more learning as the student writes. We always imagine, however, the informal writing (prewriting, journals, informal writing prompts, etc.) as places of reflexivity. Reflexivity occurs through these informal writings in a couple of ways: First, as students read and do the informal writing they should be in a space of inquiry, a space where they are questioning, asking why they think what they think, asking why they are responding to the reading in the ways that they are, and so on. Second, under your direction, students need to return to their informal writing looking for places where they encounter an earlier self or an idea that now offers a dialectical moment. The informal writing, then, acts both as a place for collecting ideas for writing within the traditional notions we have of the writing process, but also as an occasion for reflexivity. And both the dialogue journal and the dialectical notebook offer places for counter discourses (in the case of the dialogue journal, from other students or from you; in the case of the dialectical notebook, from the student at two different places in thought and time). Engaging with counter discourses is often at the heart of reflexivity.

We have chosen the readings in *Writing As Reflective Action* because we believe they offer students the opportunity to learn to read rhetorically, and reading rhetorically, we believe, is connected to the ability to write well and think analytically and critically. The "Understanding Rhetorical Strategies" sections at the end of each reading further this goal. The readings also create the potential for students to be reflective and reflexive. The readings can be confrontational for some students since they deal with conflicts between self and culture, conflicts that arise when we engage issues of race, class, and gender. It is precisely these conflicts, however, that act as powerful catalysts for engaging in reflection and reflexivity, and thus the ability to perform as active citizens in civic discourse through reading, writing, and thinking critically.

The Structure of Writing As Reflective Action

Writing As Reflective Action opens with a strong and fairly lengthy Preface that sets out several options for using the book. The Preface is followed by a detailed General Introduction to the book that explains for students what we mean by reflection, reflexivity, and action. The remainder of *Writing As Reflective Action* is in four major parts. Each builds upon previous parts while also standing as a coherent unit on its own. (We leave ample room, of course, for individual instructors to reorder readings, assignments, and even chapters to fit their own needs). Each part begins with a set of prompts for reflective prewriting followed by a short chapter introduction to help contextualize the readings and assignments. Each reading is then introduced briefly in a manner intended to provide a context for that particular piece as well as to give students some sense of direction as they read. At the end of each reading students are asked to engage in informal writing, which includes examining content, rhetorical strategies, and issues raised by the reading; they are encouraged to engage in collaborative work and to respond to prompts for further thinking about the reading just completed. Each section ends with assignment sequences which invite collaborative discussion and require students to engage in a variety of formal writing tasks. At the end of *Writing as Reflective Action* we have constructed a number of "meta" assignment sequences that draw on readings from all parts of the book, suggesting various paths through the text as a whole. Structurally, then, the text looks as follows:

I.   Preface
II.   Introduction
III.   Chapter 1
     A.   Prewriting for Chapter 1
     B.   Introduction to the chapter
     C.   Author notes for individual reading (each reading has an author note)
     D.   Individual reading (each reading follows this structure)
          1.   Reflecting on the Reading

2. Understanding Rhetorical Strategies
3. Informal Writing
E. End-of-chapter sequences

IV. Chapter 2

A. Prewriting for Chapter 2
B. Introduction to the chapter
C. Author notes for individual reading (each reading has an author note)
D. Individual reading (each reading follows this structure)
1. Reflecting on the Reading
2. Understanding Rhetorical Strategies
3. Informal Writing
E. End-of-chapter sequences

V. Chapter 3

A. Prewriting for Chapter 3
B. Introduction to the chapter
C. Author notes for individual reading (each reading has an author note)
D. Individual reading (each reading follows this structure)
1. Reflecting on the Reading
2. Understanding Rhetorical Strategies
3. Informal Writing
E. End-of-chapter sequences

VI. Chapter 4

A. Prewriting for Chapter 4
B. Introduction to the chapter
C. Sample Community-based Project A: Oral History
D. Author notes for individual reading (each reading has an author note)
E. Individual reading (each reading follows this structure)

Getting Started on the Right Foot

1.   Spend enough time on the Introduction.

We have found that treating the Introduction itself as though it were as serious a reading assignment as any of the others in the text is important. If students do not start with a basic understanding of reflection, reflexivity, and action, and how these relate to writing and thinking well in the academy and in our democratic culture, then you, as teacher, are at a distinct disadvantage and students may struggle with why they should even participate in the work of the course.

2.   Set clear outcomes and goals.

If students understand what it is you want them to learn as they work through *Writing As Reflective Action*, they are in a far better position to learn more and to produce good writing. As teachers, we far too often unintentionally mystify what it is we expect students to do.

3. Be willing to model for your students.

The critical writing, reading, and thinking that *Writing As Reflective Action* calls for is difficult and alien to many students. We have had wonderful response from our students when we take the time to model for them how to read these texts in the first couple of weeks of the term. This might mean showing them how to unravel a particularly dense or difficult passage, and then relating it to the rest of the essay, to the author's major points and ideas. Or, perhaps it means helping them locate the resources to find explanations of words and terms they don't know or understand, and to read those words within the larger rhetorical context of the essay.

4. Have your students write. A lot.

If at all possible, students should be writing daily, both in class and at home. This idea is at least as old as Horace, who is credited with the saying *"nunc dies sine lineas,"* or "never a day without a line." In other words, write every day. Every writing instructor is familiar with the formal writing assignment, but not everyone is as accustomed to making frequent use of various kinds of informal writing, whether in class (as freewrites or letters to peers), in journals of one form or another (see our Introduction for a discussion of variations on the idea of the journal), or on e-mail. This text rests on the premise that every formal essay emerges from many layers of less formal preliminary writing. This includes (and this list is not exhaustive) writing about key ideas prior to reading (Reflective Prewriting) or after reading (Reflecting on the Reading), writing to think about how writing works (Understanding Rhetorical Strategies), and writing to explore or apply ideas in preparation for more formal writing (Informal Writing). Sometimes we write to communicate something we already know, but at least as often we write to explore, to find out what we have to say on a subject. Writing is thinking. So frequent use of informal writing, while also producing the sheer volume so essential if one is to develop as a writer, also forces students to engage frequently in an especially focused kind of reflection, in *thinking*.

5. Give your students enough time.

Most experienced instructors know how to pace reading and writing assignments. Inexperienced instructors, however, are still trying to find an appropriate equilibrium. The readings in this text are long, difficult, and rich. We have found it wise to build into the syllabus a chance to reread parts, if not all, of some of the more difficult readings. Often, we will spend extra time with a text that seems critical to us for understanding and writing about a particular sequence.

6. Let your students help each other.

There are, of course, many ways in which students can work in cooperation or collaboration. Since the reading and writing assignments in *Writing As Reflective Action* are challenging, we urge you to have your students work on these readings in pairs or groups. We also urge you to make use of some form of peer critique. Students should not only know the criteria by which writing is evaluated, they should *own* and *be able to apply* those criteria. So it is a good idea to begin with an exercise that encourages your students to tell you what makes one piece of writing better, more effective than another. Regular peer critiques, whether in class or out of class (as peer response letters), give students regular opportunities to apply those criteria to actual works-in-progress. The more adept students become at applying these criteria to the writing of others, the more likely they are to be able to apply them to their own writing, to see where they themselves need to revise. But there's more: Ken Bruffee, the guru of collaborative learning, views the teacher-centered classroom featuring "the sage on the stage" as a kind of tragedy. Here's a room with twenty-five minds, only one of which is operating. And when a student speaks, all the note-takers stop taking notes: it couldn't be all that important if a student said it. In short, students need to become active learners, which means learning to take each other–and themselves–seriously, as people with ideas and points of view that matter. Peer critique enlists students in precisely this kind of practice. Then, too, there's the practical matter that when students are producing as many drafts as they need to in order to develop as writers, they produce more than most instructors can read. At least for early drafts, let students shoulder the burden.

7. Make use of the companion website for *Writing As Reflective Action*: http://www.ablongman.com/carter.

The companion website will offer links to other readings, alternative questions and exercises, a place for student interaction (asynchronous/synchronous), a place for journaling, a "contextual" glossary (providing additional examples for terms like reflexivity, reflection, etc.), additional biographical information on authors of essays, additional sample syllabi, information about researching online, and student sample papers.

Sample Syllabi

Several approaches to operationalizing *Writing As Reflective Action* are exemplified in the following syllabi. The first sample is a two-day per week, 10-week syllabus constructed by a graduate teaching associate at Ohio University. Ms. Lupo also teaches freshman writing at a community college in nearby Columbus. As you can see, Ms. Lupo's syllabus follows a basic pattern. She starts each chapter with the reflective prewriting, then follows with reading, informal writing, small group discussion, and large group discussion for each reading and the apparatus that accompanies each reading. Prior to students' engaging with the formal writing projects in the end-of-chapter sequences, she has them review all of their dialogue journals, informal writing, and notes, as well as reread the essay they found most difficult. Doing so allows students to mine their past work for ideas that they wish to carry forward into the formal writing assignment, and it sets up the possibility for students to have moments of reflexivity as they confront their earlier selves and ideas. She then has them complete the group work suggested in the end-of-chapter sequences, work that also helps prepare students for the writing assignments that follow. In this

8

particular 10-week class, Ms. Lupo has decided not to use the meta-sequences at the end of the book, but rather to use an end-of-chapter sequence from each of the chapters.

Following Ms. Lupo's syllabus as a way of offering insight into working with some of the readings in *Writing As Reflective Action*, we have included ideas for working with some of the readings from the text, those that she chose for her students. Remember, the annotations we provide are only one way of going about this. You may have better ideas.

Sample Syllabus One: Ten Weeks, 2 Times Weekly

English 151: Freshman Composition: Writing and Rhetoric Section: A47
Instructor: Marian E. Lupo
Office: Ellis 8
Office Hours: T & TH 9:30-10:30 p.m. and by appointment
Office Phone: 3-2743
Home Phone:
Email:

Texts:

Carter, Duncan and Sherrie Gradin. *Writing As Reflective Action*
Hacker, Diana. *A Writer's Reference*

Course Description:

English 151 Freshman Composition: Writing and Rhetoric focuses on writing, reading, and thinking processes. Students engage in informal writing, formal writing, peer critique, revision, active reading and group work as a means to becoming successful writers and thinkers both within and outside of the university.

When you come to college you bring your individual self, your personal history, your beliefs, your prior schooling, your regional or national origin, your rich cultural heritage. While I want to see you develop facility with academic discourses, I do not expect you to check your individual identity at the door on the way in, as you might a hat or coat. I am, therefore, especially interested in helping you explore the intersection of the personal and public, the private and social in your thinking, your reading, your writing, and your life. To come to these ends in our class, I invite you to engage in extended reflection and reflexivity, collaborative learning, informal writing and formal writing, writing for the academy. This class will ask you to explore what you know about culture (academic and otherwise) and yourself.

Specific Course Goals and Objectives:

Objectives to accomplish in this course with this text:
· Engage in reflection and reflexivity as a way of becoming better writers, readers, and thinkers.
· Engage in reflection and reflexivity as a way of understanding who we are as individuals and as members of various cultural groups.
· Engage in reflection and reflexivity as a way of thinking about and joining in civic participation.
· Use informal writing as a tool for critical thinking.
· Use informal writing as a bridge to formal, public writing.
· To gain a better understanding of the power of language and the many rhetorical strategies we use, and which are in turn used to persuade us.
· To become better thinkers, writers, and readers overall.

English Composition First-Year Program Outcome Goals For All Students:

At the end of this course students should have knowledge in the areas on the following list. It is important to remember, however, that it takes dedication and hard work from both the teacher and the student to meet these goals.

Rhetorical Knowledge
·   Identify and understand rhetorical purposes, audiences, and situations and the relationships among these
·   Understand how to draw on genre conventions to address purposes, audiences, and situations

Critical Thinking, Reading, and Writing
·   Develop their own ideas in relation to the ideas of others through writing and reading
·   Evaluate, analyze, and synthesize primary and secondary texts through writing and reading
·   Critique their own and others' ideas
·   Integrate their own with others' ideas

Processes
·   Understand writing as a recursive process that permits writers to use a variety of strategies during writing stages and processes
·   Understand the collaborative and social aspects of writing processes
·   Develop an awareness of the role of computer-mediated communication

Knowledge of Conventions
·   Practice appropriate means of documenting their work
·   Control conventions of structure, syntax, grammar, usage, punctuation, and spelling
(Adapted from *WPA Outcomes Statement for First-Year Composition, 2000*)

Course Requirements:

4 typed (formal) papers: Papers are generally 4-6 pages. Each paper will arise from our reading, informal writing, and group work. Before turning papers in for a grade, each essay will have been revised following peer critique and again following instructor feedback. When you turn your

paper in for a grade, you will include all of the informal writing, exercises and drafts that preceded the paper. Submit your material in a folder. Informal writing: This will include any in-class essays, freewriting, prewriting, response papers, or journal writing.

Conferences: You are required to attend two one-on-one conferences with the instructor. Our meeting place will be announced.

Grading:

In order to pass this class you must do all of the work, including informal writing, drafting, and peer critiques. Therefore, if you are absent during any class period where this work is taking place in the classroom, contact the instructor immediately.

Paper #1---20%
Paper #2---20%
Paper #3---20%
Paper #4---20%

Peer Critiques---10%

Informal Writing---10%

English 151 papers are graded according to the instructor's professional judgment of the overall quality of the writing and thinking, taking into account the outcome goals listed earlier and including the following: how well it fulfills the assignment; to what extent it demonstrates the principles taught in the course or expected of students entering the course; how effectively it communicates with its audience; to what extent it engages its readers; how easily it can be read and comprehended (reading ease is affected by factors such as organization, grammatical correctness, and the physical appearance of the essay); how well-developed it is; any other criteria set forth by a particular assignment.

Late papers are not accepted except under extraordinary circumstances and after prearranged negotiations with the instructor.
Absence Policy:

If you miss more than four hours of class time (e.g., two classes), your grade will lower by 1/3 for each day of absence. If you are absent, you are responsible for what you missed. Excessive tardiness will also lower your grade.

Academic Dishonesty:

Plagiarism is defined by the Ohio University Student Handbook as a Code A offense, which means that "[a] student found to have violated any of the following regulations will be subject to a maximum sanction of expulsion, or any sanction not less than a reprimand. Plagiarism involves the presentation of some other person's work as if it were the work of the presenter. A faculty member has the authority to grant a failing grade as well as referring the case to the director of judiciaries" (10). Any student that has chosen to plagiarize will receive a failing grade for the course. Thus, if you are unsure about plagiarism or what it means, talk with your instructor.

Civil Discourse, Rights, and Responsibilities:

In our class discussion, in our readings, and in our writing throughout this quarter, we will be examining ideas from diverse perspectives. At this university, students and faculty are afforded an academic environment that allows for intellectual expression; challenging issues and ideas may arise, but none of these should be expressed in an inappropriate manner either verbally or in writing. One of the goals of a university is to challenge us to think again about what we know (and all that we don't know). This demands that we all share responsibility for creating and maintaining a civil learning environment in our classrooms and in the larger university community. This means that we will be conscious of and accept responsibility for what we say and do, how we act, how our words and actions have consequences, and how our words and actions affect others.

As part of this awareness we will avoid sexist, racist, and heterosexist language. We will not perpetuate stereotypes.
Official University "No Class" Days:
Veteran's Day: Friday, November 10
Reading Day: Wednesday, November 15
Last Day of Classes: Tuesday, November 14

Tentative Schedule

Week 1, 9/5 & 9/7

T   Introduction to course and explanation of syllabus
In class writing: Reflective Prewriting for Chapter 1
Discussion/lecture on writing process models
Homework--Reading Assignment: Introduction to the textbook
Homework--Reading Assignment: Introduction to Part I and Iserhoff, "Excerpts From My Life"
Writing Assignment: Dialogue Journal response on Reflecting on the Reading (immediately following the Iserhoff essay)
Homework--Writing Assignment: Answer, as thoroughly as possible, the prompts under Informal Writing (following the Iserhoff essay)

TH   Guided Freewriting: What do you still have questions about from your reading of the Introduction?
Share from freewrites and discussion of the Introduction
Further discussion/lecture on writing process models (if needed)
Dialogue Journal Exchange (15 minutes)
Group Work: Understanding Rhetorical Strategies (following the Iserhoff essay) (20 minutes)
Large Group Discussion (40 minutes)
Share and discuss writing done for Informal Writing prompts
Completion of discussion on Iserhoff
Homework--Reading Assignment: Robert Coles, "Entitlement"
Writing: Dialogue Journal response on Reflecting on the Reading
Homework--Writing Assignment: Answer, as thoroughly as possible, the prompts under Informal Writing

Week 2, 9/12 & 9/14

T   Dialogue Journal Exchange (15 minutes)
Group Work: Understanding Rhetorical Strategies (20 minutes)
Large Group Discussion (40 minutes)
Class discussion of Informal Writing prompts and Coles essay
Homework--Reading Assignment: hooks, "Killing Rage"
Writing Assignment: Dialogue Journal response to Reflecting on the
Reading
Homework--Writing Assignment: Answer, as thoroughly as
possible, the prompts under Informal Writing

TH   Large class discussion on "Killing Rage" (40 minutes)
Group Work: Understanding Rhetorical Strategies (20 minutes)
Large group follow up on Understanding Rhetorical Strategies (10
minutes)
Group Work from End-of-chapter Sequence Two: Cultural Blindness
(ignore "Boys Will Be Men")
Homework--Reading Assignment: 1) Reread all dialogue journals,
informal writing, and notes you've written on the Iserhoff, Coles, and
hooks essays. 2) Reread the essay that was most difficult for you of the
three essays.
Writing Assignment: Write a complete draft of Paper #1 based on prompt
#1 from Sequence Two: Cultural Blindness.

Week 3, 9/19 & 9/21

T   Complete Draft of Paper #1 due for peer critique (make two
copies, one to submit to instructor)
Reflective Prewriting to Chapter 2
Read and discuss Introduction to Chapter 2
Sign-up for Thursday conferences (ten students)
Conferences
Homework--Revising draft

Homework--Reading Assignment: Steinem, "Ruth's Song"
Writing Assignment: Dialogue Journal response to Reflecting on the
Reading

TH   2nd draft of Paper #1 due to Instructor
Mini-workshop on writing issue and catch up
Conferences
Dialogue Journal Exchange (15 minutes)
Group Work: Understanding Rhetorical Strategies (20 minutes)
Large Group Discussion (15 minutes)
In-class writing: Informal Writing Prompts for "Ruth's Song"
Large Class Discussion (40 minutes)
Homework--Reading Assignment: Robinson, "The Hurt, Betrayed Son"
Writing Assignment: Dialogue Journal response to Reflecting on the
Reading
Homework--Reading Assignment: Villanueva, "An American of Color"
Writing Assignment: Dialogue Journal response to Reflecting on the
Reading

Week 4, 9/26 & 9/28

T   **Pick up Instructor comments on 2nd draft of Paper #1
(everybody)
Dialogue Journal Exchange for "The Hurt, Betrayed Son" and for "An
American of Color" (30 minutes)
Group Work: Understanding Rhetorical Strategies for both essays (40
minutes)
Large Group Discussion of Robinson & Villanueva (30 minutes)
Homework--Revising Draft #2 of Paper #1

TH   Final Draft of Paper #1 due (Remember to include all of the
informal writing, exercises and drafts that preceded the paper. Submit
your material in a folder.)
In-class essay (bullet 3 from Reflecting on the Reading) (30 minutes)
Large class discussion of the in-class essay answers and other Reflecting
on the Reading bullets

In-class writing: writing on prompts from Informal Writing
Group Work from End-of-chapter Sequence Two: Self vs. Role.
Homework--Reading Assignment: 1) Reread all dialogue journals,
informal writing, and notes you've written on the Steinem, Robinson, and
Villanueva essays. 2) Reread the essay that was most difficult for you of
the three essays.
Writing Assignment: Write a complete draft of Paper #2 based on prompt
#3 from Sequence Two: Self vs. Role.

Week 5, 10/3 & 10/5

T   Complete Draft of Paper #2 for peer critique (make two copies,
one to submit to instructor); Turn in all Dialogue Journal Responses
Mini-workshop on writing issues and catch up
Reflective Pre-writing to Chapter 3
Read Introduction to Chapter 3 and discussion of Introduction to
Chapter 3
Homework--Reading Assignment: Tompkins, "Me and My Shadow"
Writing Assignment: Dialogue Journal response to Reflecting on the
Reading
Homework--Revising Draft #1 of Paper #2

TH   2nd Draft of Paper #2 to Instructor
Dialogue Journal Exchange (15 minutes)
Group Work: Understanding Rhetorical Strategies (20 minutes)
Large Group Discussion (15 minutes)
In-class writing: Informal Writing Prompts for "Me and My Shadow"
Large Class Discussion (40 minutes)
Homework--Reading Assignment: Williams, "The Brass Ring and the
Deep Blue Sea"
Writing Assignment: Dialogue Journal response to Reflecting on the
Reading
Homework--Reading Assignment: Geertz, "'From the Native's Point of
View': On the Nature of Anthropological Understanding"
Writing Assignment: Dialogue Journal Response to Reflecting on the
Reading

Week 6, 10/10 & 10/12

T   **Pick up Instructor comments on 2nd Draft of Paper #2
Dialogue Journal Exchange for "The Brass Ring and the Deep Blue Sea"
and "'From the Native's Point of View'" (30 minutes)
Group Work: Understanding Rhetorical Strategies for both essays (40 minutes)
Large Group Discussion of Williams and Geertz (30 minutes)
Homework--Revise Draft #2 of Paper #2

TH   Final Draft of Paper #2 to Instructor (Remember to include all of the informal writing, exercises and drafts that preceded the paper. Submit your material in a folder.)
In-class essay (from Reflecting on the Reading) (30 minutes)
Large class discussion of the in-class essay answers and other Reflecting on the Reading bullets
In-class writing: writing on prompts from Informal Writing
Sign-up for Tuesday conferences (ten students)
Group Work from End-of-chapter Sequence Four: Private or Public (ignore "Tlilli, Tlapalli: The Path of the Red and Black Ink")
Homework--Reading Assignment: 1) Reread all dialogue journals, informal writing, and notes you've written on the Tompkins, Williams, and Geertz essays. 2) Reread the essay that was most difficult for you of the three essays.
Writing Assignment: Write a complete draft of Paper #3 based on prompt #1 from Sequence Four: Private or Public.

Week 7, 10/17 & 10/19

T   Complete Draft of Paper #3 due for peer critique (make two copies, one to submit to instructor)
Mini-workshop on writing issues and catch up
Reflective Pre-writing to Chapter 4
Read Introduction to Chapter 4 and discussion of Introduction to

Chapter 4
Sign-up for Thursday conferences (ten students)
Conferences
Homework--Reading Assignment: Studs Terkel, "Working the Land"
Writing Assignment: Dialogue Journal response to Reflecting on the Reading
Homework--Revising Draft #1 of Paper #3

TH   2nd Draft of Paper #3 to Instructor
Dialogue Journal Exchange (15 minutes)
Group Work: Understanding Rhetorical Strategies (20 minutes)
Large Group Discussion (15 minutes)
In-class writing: Informal Writing Prompts for "Working the Land"
Large Class Discussion (40 minutes)
Conferences
Homework--Reading Assignment: Terry, "Private First Class Reginald 'Malik' Edwards, Phoenix, Louisiana"
Writing Assignment: Dialogue Journal response to Reflecting on the Reading
Homework--Reading Assignment (in Part III): Gibson, "Paintball as Combat Sport"
Writing Assignment: Dialogue Journal Response to Reflecting on the Reading

Week 8, 10/24 & 10/26

T   **Pick up Instructor comments on 2nd Draft of Paper #3 (everybody)
Dialogue Journal Exchange for "Private First Class Reginald 'Malik' Edwards, Phoenix, Louisiana" and "Paintball as Combat Sport'" (30 minutes)
Group Work: Understanding Rhetorical Strategies for both essays (40 minutes)
Large Group Discussion of Terry and Gibson (30 minutes)
Homework--Revising Draft #2 of Paper #3

TH   Final Draft of paper #3 due to Instructor (Remember to include all of the informal writing, exercises and drafts that preceded the paper. Submit your material in a folder.)
In-class essay (from Reflecting on the Reading) (30 minutes)
Large class discussion of the in-class essay answers and other Reflecting on the Reading bullets
In-class writing: writing on prompts from Informal Writing
Group Work from End-of-chapter Sequence Three: History and the Individual (ignore "Violet De Cristoforo")
Homework--Reading Assignment: 1) Reread all dialogue journals, informal writing, and notes you've written on the Terkel, Terry, and Gibson essays. 2) Reread the essay that was most difficult for you of the three essays.
Writing Assignment: Write a complete draft of Paper #4 based on prompt #1 from Sequence Three: History and the Individual.

Week 9, 10/31 & 11/2

T   Complete Draft of Paper #4 due for peer critique (make two copies, one to submit to instructor)
Mini-workshop on writing issues and catch up
Homework--Revising Draft #1 of Paper #4

TH   2nd Draft of Paper #4 to Instructor
Homework--TBA

Week 10, 11/7 & 11/9

T   **Pick up Instructor comments on 2nd Draft of Paper #4 (everybody)
Homework--Revising Draft #2 of Paper #4

TH   Final Draft of paper #4 due to Instructor (Remember to include all of the informal writing, exercises and drafts that preceded the paper. Submit your material in a folder.)
Turn in all remaining Dialogue Journal Reponses

Week 11   Exam Week--TBA

Discussion of Selected Readings

Ideas for the Readings included in Ms. Lupo's Syllabus

Annie Neeposh Iserhoff: "Excerpts From My Life"
Students generally connect readily to Iserhoff's essay because it is a straightforward personal essay, a form that seems quite familiar and comfortable to them. Because they are so comfortable, however, our experience has taught us that students also want to read it in an uncomplicated manner.

We find the informal writing and small group discussions helpful as a way of beginning to complicate a student's initial reading of Iserhoff's piece. Ms. Lupo's syllabus asks students to keep a dialogue journal, primarily focusing on the Reflecting on the Reading and Informal Writing prompts. As homework, then, her students respond to those prompts (on half of an 8-1/2 x 11 sheet of paper—see the Introduction to WRA) and bring the responses to class to share with a dialogue partner. The first task of the class period focusing on Iserhoff is to exchange journals. This allows students, through an informal writing space, to exchange initial ideas on the questions raised in the Reflecting on the Reading section. This works well whether one is teaching in a computer classroom or a more traditional setting. An alternative approach that also works well is to have students do this outside of class time through e-mail.

Because the sections on Rhetorical Strategies often seem to raise concepts and ideas that students are less familiar with say, as in the case of the Iserhoff prompts, how tone and diction relate to her content, we have found that it works well for students to work in small groups, sharing their ideas prior to a large group discussion. If allotted class time does not allow for each group to work on every prompt, it also works well to assign just one of the prompts to each group.

While you might sometimes feel that the informal writing and small group discussions have been productive enough in terms of your goals for the reading and writing, as a general rule, we like to engage the class in full class discussion following informal writing, small group discussion, or both. We expect that informal writing (especially dialogue journals and dialectical notebooks) and small group discussions have afforded some counter discourse (alternate points of view) to arise; we find that both the teacher and other groups offer many more counter discourses to help students find reflective and reflexive moments. Full class discussion is also a nice way to end a class session by letting many voices speak in a culminating moment.

Robert Coles: "Entitlement"
Coles's "Entitlement" clearly shifts students into reading, writing, and thinking about an academic piece. At the same time, students seem to make many connections to this work in ways they don't some of the other, less narrative, academic writings in *Writing as Reflective Action*. "Entitlement" is in some ways a perfect reading to illustrate for students how to raise questions about methodology, cultural programming, and reflexivity. Coles's ethnographic approach to a question of psychological entitlement puts both himself as researcher and the students as readers into a prime position to be reflexive since reflexivity is at the heart of any cultural ethnography. Students may need help from you as the instructor in identifying these moments of reflexivity, however, especially if you choose to use "Entitlement" early in the term.

As you can see, Ms. Lupo chooses to follow the same pattern of dialogue journal response to Reflecting on the Reading, small group discussion on Understanding Rhetorical Strategies, and informal writing.

bell hooks: "Killing Rage"
"Killing Rage" elicits strong reactions from students. Many students are convinced that she was seriously on the brink of committing murder. Others believe she is making too much of a small incident that had nothing to do with race. Still others are angry with her for making them feel

guilty. Some, especially minority students, understand both hooks's reaction and her call for anger as a mode of constructive action.

One of the few places that Ms. Lupo breaks the pattern of starting with student dialogue exchanges and small group discussions is with this essay (see week 2, 9/12 and 9/14, TH). Instead, she begins with large group discussion. She does so because we find that the students immediately begin to support each others' reading of hooks as homicidal and unreasonable. For various reasons, the counter discourses to this interpretation are rare, and the initial reactionary readings tend to become reified without teacher intervention with alternate points of view early on. Ms. Lupo then moves students into groups to focus on the Rhetorical Strategies prompts. Having students discuss the rhetorical aspects of the essay also seems to ease students from those earlier gut reactions to an understanding of hooks's rhetorical positioning.

While the strong student reactions to "Killing Rage" can be disconcerting, this essay allows for (doesn't guarantee) one of the most powerful reflexive experiences of the entire text.

Gloria Steinem: "Ruth's Song (Because She Could Not Sing It)"
This is one of our favorite essays and one that students like as well. Unless students read the author introduction (and a surprising number don't, even though they are asked to), many are unaware that Gloria Steinem is a longtime leader of feminist thought. Thus, their first reading of "Ruth's Song" tends to ignore the feminist critique of patriarchy and instead centers on the narrative of mental illness and Gloria's relationship with her mother. They find themselves engaged with and moved by Steinem's narrative. The reading, writing, and group prompts that accompany "Ruth's Song," however, do work to open students to Steinem's other points about patriarchal control of women. Students are often pleasantly surprised that such a strong public critique was made through Steinem's private experiences. "Ruth's Song" works well to help students begin to close the gap between their own private and public selves.

23

While Ms. Lupo's 10-week syllabus as currently conceived may not allow for it, a very interesting and productive dialectic and counter discourse can occur when you have students do the fourth prompt under Informal Writing following "Ruth's" Song and the third prompt under Informal Writing, following "The Hurt Betrayed Son." Both prompts ask students to interview men and women informally and collect their stories and definitions of womanhood and manhood.

Doug Robinson: "The Hurt Betrayed Son"
While we don't usually find students who have read the Rambo novels, and fewer and fewer students who have seen the movies, almost all of them have heard the name Rambo. Usually more than one student has named or known a pet called Rambo. And almost all know the rhetorical intent behind calling a pet or a person Rambo. The fact that Rambo has entered American culture without critique helps make "The Hurt, Betrayed Son" an interesting and useful read for students. They find themselves intrigued by Robinson's thesis that *First Blood* and the other movies and novels might be about male sensitivity and transformation, and that Rambo might actually be a positive role model for young men.

However, students do seem to have difficulty with this piece because it is a chapter from a book. Robinson refers to previous arguments and interpretive readings (on *Spenser for Hire*, for instance) and this seems to confuse students. Also, they need to understand that Robinson is using *First Blood* as evidence in a larger argument. Thus, they need help from the instructor in knowing how to deal with references from the other chapters and how to read this chapter as both evidence within a larger argument and as an argument in itself.

Robinson's exploratory reading of Rambo opens the door for discussion on the social construction of gender, on ways in which individuals might resist that construction, on cultural critiques, and on how Robinson's academic enterprise might or might not be a stab at reflexivity. Placing Robinson's text in conversation with Steinem's is a natural move. Concepts about cultural programming and father/son and mother/daughter relationships thread their way through both essays. It is also interesting to discuss these two essays in light of audience and author positioning. Steinem is a public figure, not an academic, writing for a popular audience. Robinson is an academic figure, writing as an academic for an academic audience, but his book *No Less A Man,* from which "The Hurt, Betrayed Son" comes, was published by Bowling Green University's Popular Press Series. Both essays use private experience to make public arguments.

Victor Villanueva: "An American of Color"
At first glance, students are usually unsure about what to make of Villanueva's piece. They seem to like his personal stories, but don't always readily make the connection from that private experience to his public arguments about the minority and the immigrant and the experience of colonialism. We have found close study of the questions raised under Understanding Rhetorical Strategies helpful to students' understanding of Villaneuva's rich argument. We have also found paying close attention to Villaneuva's discussion of the melting pot and other metaphors of assimilation helps students understand Villaneuva's aim. Unraveling these various metaphors also places students in the stream of a dialectic necessary to experience their own reflexivity. Having students come up with their own metaphors (something other than the melting pot) has also proven to be a workable framework from which students can begin a discussion of the issues raised in "An American of Color."

Jane Tompkins: "Me and My Shadow"
Jane Tompkins's essay seems to elicit strong response on each end of a continuum. Students struggle to understand the point of her essay, feeling helpless and frustrated, or they get behind her, cheering her for the challenge to what they see as boring academic writing. We have seen few students who are just ho-hum in their responses. It is true that many more students are frustrated and unhappy than are her cheerleaders. We do not see this as unfortunate, however, but rather as a real opportunity to work through a difficult piece together. When we do have a number of students who are negative about this essay, we have found it useful to try the following to get students started:

Write these five questions on the board (leaving room for students to write underneath them later): 1) Why (why not) is literature important? 2) Why (why not) is literary criticism/theory important? 3) What is Tompkins's feeling about literary criticism/theory? 4) What is one thing you understand about this essay? 5) What is one thing you don't understand about this essay? Have students informally write about each of these questions for a total of fifteen to twenty minutes.

When they are finished writing, count the students off by fours, asking each one to come to the board and write down one idea under the corresponding number. These lists offer the grounding for a large-group discussion. Following a large-group discussion, we like to have students come to consensus on what they think Tompkins's major point is and then write it out in three or fewer sentences. Holding that consensus understanding of Tompkins's essay in front of them, we send them back to work on the prompts following the reading.

Tompkins's double voicing is also something that draws ire from some students. Here is one student's response: "It seems to me that Tompkins switches topics a lot in this essay. I didn't really understand the point of writing the article . . . I didn't get why she was struggling to figure out whether to write in academic writing or not." When student responses such as this arise, several things have proven effective in bringing students into conversation with this particular text. First, a careful class reading of the author introduction helps those frustrated students understand the framework and context from which Tompkins is writing. While the prompts at the end of the text are invaluable in helping students unravel this essay, the overly frustrated student has often given up and therefore resisted working honestly with the prompts. Taking time to work carefully through the prompts, especially the Reflecting on the Reading prompts, may be time consuming, but in this case it is time well spent. The Reflecting on the Reading prompts directly address the context for the essay and the reason for Tompkins's double voicing. Finally, we suggest rereading Tompkins through Williams's multiple voicing in "The Brass Ring and the Deep Blue Sea" (see the comments on Williams's essay).

26

Patricia Williams: "The Brass Ring and the Deep Blue Sea"
While students find "The Brass Ring and the Deep Blue Sea" difficult, they generally like it and are willing to try to follow Williams's use of multiple voices as they relate to her critique of the law. Since students, for the most part, are less willing to accept Tompkins's double voice, we have found it a natural to ask them to examine their seemingly contradictory responses. Within this framework, it becomes fairly easy to engage students with the concept of reflexivity by asking them to read Tompkins's double voicing through Williams's multiple voicing, and then, based on what they learn, read their own initial reactions to Tompkins and Williams. Of course, reflexivity is more than just reading one text through the lens of another text. Reflexivity requires a willingness to step into a different perspective, allowing for dialectic to arise.

Because students tend to focus on Williams's story of the little boy and the dogs, and her slide through the rabbit hole to talk with her sister, these two passages are good leverage points into the essay. If students can begin to understand these passages, they can begin to understand both how Williams's work is reflexive and how she creates a subject position by which to critique the discipline of law, a discipline that under most circumstances would deny her a subject position at all.

Wallace Terry: "Private First Class Reginald 'Malik' Edwards, Phoenix, Louisiana"
This is another essay that students say they enjoy reading. Yet, they are often shocked at the graphic representation of Private Edwards's memories. They are taken aback that he had to go through the things he did. After all, most eighteen-year-olds in our classrooms are Americans who barely remember the Gulf War (if they remember it at all). And what they know of that war seems so much more "clean" and "antiseptic" than what Malik Edwards shares with them.

We have had exceptional luck starting students in one of two places with this text. The first prompt under Reflecting on the Reading that asks students to examine the absurdities and paradoxes that Edwards writes about seems to offer a conceptual framework from which to read the account.   Also, the third prompt under Understanding Rhetorical Strategies that draws students' attention to Edwards's references to popular media works to underscore the differences between Edwards's eye account and the idea of war in the popular imagination and the students' imaginations. Reading the opening paragraph carefully and asking why it seemed such a big deal to Edwards that Morely Safer was there with him helps students better understand Edwards's relationship to and with the happenings he either observed or participated in.

As is often the case, it is also helpful to have students compare the oral historians' approaches to their subjects as well. Asking to work through the end-of-reading prompts seems fun to students in this case, and they seem eager to re-engage with the text.

James William Gibson: "Paintball As Combat Sport"
In ending with Gibson's "Paintball," Ms. Lupo has circled back to Chapter III, "The Self and Others: Reflexivity." Students find Gibson's essay a fairly easy read, especially if they have already grappled with Tompkins, Williams, and Geertz. Often, students take two different positions: one, that Gibson is arguing that playing paintball is a good thing for men and for curbing real violence in the world; and two, that Gibson is arguing that paintball causes aggression, violence, and a lusting for war among men who play it. Asking students to defend their readings and playing these two defenses against each other proves fruitful. So, too, does taking what Geertz argues about conducting anthropological inquiry and seeing how Gibson's cultural study and his subjectivity stack up against Geertz's arguments.

Clifford Geertz: "'From the Native's Point of View': On the Nature of Anthropological Understanding"
This is a difficult selection for students. They tend to get bogged down in the profusion of detail Geertz provides in his portraits of the sense of selfhood in three different cultures. One way to approach this article is by viewing it as a relatively conventional academic essay, meaning, in this case, that it begins with the conventional wisdom about X, then proceeds to explain what is wrong with that position. The question for students,

28

then, is what is the conventional wisdom that Geertz targets in this piece (the belief that anthropologists must be highly empathetic in order to understand "the natives' point of view."). Instead, Geertz argues, anthropologists come to understand and interpret other cultures through a method which involves "a continuous dialectical tacking between the most local of local detail and the most global of global structure in such a way as to bring them into simultaneous view."

If students can come to understand what view Geertz is critiquing, and what he is offering in its place, they have won half the battle. One way to nudge them in this direction is to ask them–singly or in small groups–to explain what Geertz means by the last sentence of the essay. If this is not an adequate nudge, ask students to explain Geertz's analogies, comparing the process of understanding a culture with the process of understanding a baseball game, or a poem (Understanding Rhetorical Strategies, #4).

Two particularly fruitful questions for thinking or writing about Geertz: (1) How does his style relate to what he has to say about anthropological method? (Understanding Rhetorical Strategies, #3). (2) How does Geertz's essay relate to the concept of reflexivity, especially since he seems to rule out the necessity of empathy? (Reflecting on the Reading, #1).

Sample Syllabus Two: 10 Weeks, 2 Times Weekly, Focused Primarily on a Single Chapter (Chapter II—Self as Social Artifact)

This syllabus imagines a 10-week, quarter system course in which students write five major essays, culminating in a final portfolio. (Some instructors may prefer to slow things down, working through more drafts; alternatively, by doing little more than adding a third draft of every essay, instructors on the semester system could easily expand it to a semester-length course.) Students read all of the essays in Chapter 2, bracketed by one essay from Chapter 1 (Updike) and one from Chapter 3 (Tompkins). The thematic focus of the course on the concept of self vs. role works something like this: Updike presents a thoughtful reflection on the self, dramatizing the familiar notion that we can think of ourselves as more or less autonomous individuals. The essays of Chapter 2 complicate this notion, suggesting in one way or another that while there may be such a thing as an individual self, there is much about the self that is shaped by the society in which we find ourselves. If we have selves, we also have roles, and the selves don't always fit the roles. The essays in Chapter 2 permit extensive exploration of the permutations and complications of this theme. Concluding with Tompkins extends this theme into the academic arena (and thus to the problems of academic writing, including the students' own academic writing) and introduces the concept of reflexivity. While the fact that our selves are socially constructed may seem a negative in some respects, our social situation can also, through reflexivity, lead to significant growth, even transformation.

My students do a lot more writing than the syllabus below suggests. I draw heavily upon reflective prewriting, reflecting on the reading, understanding rhetorical strategies, and informal writing prompts as time and the direction of the class permit. I also assign a journal, usually an email journal shared by the entire class, which requires students to respond to the readings and to each other at least three times a week (with a minimal entry defined as 100 words), or 30 entries for the term. Journals are graded on quantity and regularity only.

Week One

M Introduction to the course
  Freewriting/Focused Freewriting
  Reflective Prewriting: Chapter 1, prompt #1 (conceptual turning
   points–self-reflection)
  For Wednesday: Read Updike

  Updike, "On Being a Self Forever"
  Reflecting on the Reading: Focused Freewrite, prompt #1 or
   prompt #2 (apparent contradiction; effect of encounters on
   self)
  Class discussion

For Friday: Informal writing in response to prompt #2,
Understanding Rhetorical Strategies (Updike's use of personal
stories)
Re-read Updike

F   Updike, continued
Group discussion: Reflecting on the Reading, prompt #3 (which
episodes important, definition of manhood)–25 minutes
Class discussion–25 minutes

Note: When I begin with group discussion, I usually devote about half the period to that activity, then open it up to a whole-class discussion. This is my favorite sequence: The individual freewrites or writes journal entry, shares it in group discussion, then participates in a whole-class discussion. This sequence discourages group-think by forcing each individual to collect his/her own thoughts first, before discussion, and gives the shy an opportunity to test the waters in small groups before plunging into a larger discussion.

For Monday: Draft #1 of paper #1 due (from end-of-chapter
sequence 3, prompt #2—how we use stories to make sense
of our lives). Bring four copies.

Week Two

M   Draft #1 of paper #1 due
Peer response in groups

Note: Often it is a good idea to spend a whole period preparing students to do peer response, eliciting criteria from them and modeling how to apply those criteria.

For Wednesday: Write in response to any of the prompts under
Reflective Prewriting, Chapter 2
Read Introduction to Chapter 2, "Self as Social Artifact"
Read Steinem

W   Steinem, "Ruth's Song (Because She Could not Sing It)"
Reflecting on the Reading, Focused Freewrite: prompt #1 or #3
      (comparisons of Ruth to uncle, to other women in her life)
Class discussion
For Friday: Read Robinson
      Write in response to any of the prompts under Reflecting
      on the Reading or Understanding Rhetorical Strategies

F   Robinson, "The Hurt, Betrayed Son"
Group discussion: all three prompts, Reflecting on the Reading–25
      minutes
Class discussion–25 minutes
For Monday: Draft #2 of paper #1 due

Week Three

M   Works-in-Progress

Note: Discussion of 3 or 4 student papers, drawn from draft #1 of assignment one. What's here that you like? What needs to be revised? If I have had students develop their own set of criteria for peer response, I use them here. I like to do this because (a) writing by their peers rivets student attention, (b) I can establish a good number of rhetorical issues through these samples, and (c) I like to avoid assigning reading the day a paper is due. Otherwise, I sometimes find myself having a one-person discussion.

W   Class discussion, Steinem and Robinson, continued
For Friday: Read Villanueva
      Write in response to any of the prompts under Reflecting
      on the Reading or Understanding Rhetorical Strategies

F   Villaneuva, "An American of Color"
Group discussion: Reflecting on the Reading, one prompt to each
      group

For Monday: Draft #1 of paper #2 due (end-of-chapter sequence 2, prompt #1–conflict between self and role)

Week Four

M   Villaneuva, continued
      Class discussion
      Draft #1 of paper #2 due. Bring four copies.
      For Wednesday: take-home peer response letters due

W   Revising structure

Note: Usually I use an associatively organized (or "writer-based") student draft, ask students to identify the structural problems, then show them how to reverse outline as a step toward global revision.

      Take-home peer response letters due
      For Friday: Read Rich
             Write in response to any of the prompts under Reflecting
             on the Reading or Understanding Rhetorical Strategies

F   Rich, "The Domestication of Motherhood"
      Group discussion: Reflecting on the Reading, one prompt to each
             group
      For Monday: Draft #2 of paper #2 due
      Reread Rich

Week Five

M   Rich, continued
      Class discussion
      Draft #2 of paper #2 due

W   Exercises in revision
      What a reflective cover letter looks like

For Friday: bring four copies of a paper you are revising for the mid-term portfolio

F   Workshop: Peer Response and Revision
        For Monday: Mid-term portfolio due

Week Six

M   Examination of Sample Drafts
        Mid-term portfolio due
        For Wednesday: Read Rust
                Write in response to any of the prompts under Reflecting on the Reading or Understanding Rhetorical Strategies

W   Rust, "Sexual Identity and Bisexual Identities"
        Group discussion: Reflecting on the Reading, one prompt to a group
        For Friday: Reread Rust

F   Rust, continued
        Class discussion
        For Monday: Draft #1 of paper #3 due (end-of-chapter sequence 3, Prompt #2–process of social construction). Bring four copies.

Week Seven

M   Rust, continued
        Focused Freewrite: Meta-sequence #1, prompt #2 (using Rust's process to describe self-definition in aspects of identity other than the sexual)
        Class discussion
        Draft #1 of paper #3 due. Bring four copies.
        For Wednesday: Peer response letters due

W   Writing-in-Progress

Peer response letters due
For Friday: Draft #2 of paper #3 due.

F   Class discussion: Taking Stock—Where are we on the concept of
self vs. role? The process of social construction?
Draft #2 of paper #3 due
For Monday: Read Tompkins

Week Eight

M   Tompkins, "Me and My Shadow"
Class discussion based on prompts under Reflecting on the
Reading
For Wednesday: Draft #1 of paper #4 due. Bring four copies.

W   Tompkins, continued
Class discussion based on prompts under Understanding Rhetorical
Strategies and Informal Writing
Draft #1 of paper #4 due–Meta-sequence #1, prompt #2 (using
Rust's process to describe self-definition in some aspect of
your own identity other than the sexual)

F   Writing-in-Progress
For Monday: Draft #2 of paper #4 due

Week Nine

M   Tompkins, continued
Class discussion. Consider: How does Tompkins relate to the
essays we've read from Chapter 2 and the issues we have
discussed subsequent to reading them?
Draft #2 of paper #4 due
For Wednesday: Read the Introductions to Chapters 2 and 3

W   Class Discussion: Self, Role, and Reflexivity
(based in part on Introductions to Chapters 2 and 3)

Note: Here we continue working toward a synthesis, or synthes*es*, a process we began Monday. I hope we will arrive at something like the idea that while the self's status as a social artifact may seem–even be–limiting in certain respects (as when the role one is called upon to play doesn't seem to fit the self), the fact that we are socially situated can be used to our advantage (growth, expanded awareness, new perspectives) through reflexivity.

For Friday: Draft #1 of paper #5 due

F   To Be Announced
     Draft #1 of paper #5 due. Bring four copies.

Note: I would select–or design–this assignment in accordance with the direction the class has taken up to this point, but it is likely to be something along the lines of the way Tompkins complicates the idea of self vs. role, self vs. role in academic writing, or Tompkins, reflexivity, and the social construction of self.

For Monday: Peer response letters due

Week Ten

M   Writing-in-Progress
     Peer response letters due.
     For Wednesday: Bring drafts of reflective cover letters and/or
          papers you are planning to revise for inclusion in your final
          portfolio

W   Workshop
     Draft #2 of paper #5 due. Bring four copies.
     For Friday: Bring drafts of reflective cover letters and/or papers
          you are planning to revise for inclusion in your final
          portfolio

Finals Week

Final portfolio due (To include reflective cover letter of 4-6 pages, three revised papers, and two pieces of informal writing–or freewriting, or email.)

Sample Syllabus Three: 15 weeks, 3 Times Weekly, With Community-based Component

This sample syllabus illustrates a course fifteen weeks long with three one-hour classes per week. The course integrates three community-based projects into the last ten weeks of the course. During the first five weeks, students work with reading and writing selections from Chapters 1, 2, and 3. Students complete two formal writing assignments, one from the sequences at the end of Chapter 1, and one from the Meta-Sequences at the end of the text, by the start of the seventh week. Informal writing centers around the dialectical notebook (see the Introduction to WRA), the triple-entry incident journal (see the Introduction to Chapter 4), and the informal writing prompts following the readings.

Beginning the sixth week, students start working on their community-based projects by creating a Code of Conduct that will guide their interactions and collective behavior with their community partners. In the seventh week, students begin spending time with their community partners. Two groups of students work with partners who need tutoring or learning support (ABLE and Head Start). One group works with a partner who needs a grant written (Education Cooperative).

In the final seven weeks of the course, the students charged with the tutoring work must complete (including peer critique sessions) the following three projects: social analysis and commentary; reflective and reflexive narrative; and an assessment of the community-based project. During this time, the group of students working with the Education Cooperative to complete a grant submission must complete (including peer critique sessions) the following projects: the grant proposal for the community partner; a social analysis and commentary OR a reflective and reflexive narrative; and an assessment of the community-based project. All groups must also build in two more sets (three entries) of triple-entry incident journal responses. As set up in this syllabus, the groups themselves, with the approval of the instructor, set a timeline for drafting, peer critiquing, and completing each of these assignments. The instructor provides feedback on each writing assignment as well. At the final exam meeting students will turn in the final versions of the writing assignments tied to their community-based project.

Freshman English: MWF 11-12
Section 15
Instructor: S. Gradin
Office: Basement, Scott Quad
Office hours: TTH 10-12 and by appointment

Please be aware that if you stay in this section of Freshman English you will be committing to a writing course that includes a community-based project. This means that you will be working with an already identified agency outside of the university. You will be involved either in tutoring or grant writing. We will discuss this part of the course in detail during class time on the first two days of the course.

Textbooks: *Writing As Reflective Action* (Carter and Gradin) and *The Scott Foresman Handbook* (Ruszkiewicz, Hairston, and Seward)

Course Assignments:
Informal Writing (prompts, notebooks, journals, peer critiques): 10%
Formal Essay #1: 20%
Formal Essay #2: 20%
*Community-based Collection of Writing: 50%

*Those of you who will be tutoring will have the following three projects due for this collection: social analysis and commentary; reflective and reflexive narrative; and an assessment of the community-based project. Those of you working with the Education Cooperative will have the following projects due for this collection: the grant proposal for the community partner; a social analysis and commentary OR a reflective and reflexive narrative; and an assessment of the community-based project. We will discuss in class the perimeters of these writing projects and how they will be graded as a holistic whole.

Attendance Policy: The work that goes on in this classroom is often not replicable outside of class, nor is it retrievable from lecture notes or textbooks. Thus, attendance is mandatory. If you miss more than three unexcused class periods, your grade will drop a full letter grade. For each class you miss after three, your grade will continue to drop a letter grade.

Plagiarism: Plagiarism or cheating of any kind is not tolerated by the university (see attached handout from the Student Handbook).

Tentative Schedule and Due Dates

WEEK 1
Mon -- Course Introduction: Writing as process; writing as revision; writing as reading and thinking
5-hr. commitment to the community project
Homework: Introduction to WRA

Wed -- Guided Writing: "Questions I have after reading the Introduction"
Discussion of Introduction
Introduction to the Dialectical Notebook
Homework: Reflective Prewriting for Chapter 1

Fri -- Continued discussion of important terms from the Introduction. Discussion and outline of community-based learning project. Determining your project partner: ABLE Adult Education Program; Tri-County Community Action (The Plains Head Start); or Southeastern Ohio Voluntary Education Cooperative.
Homework: Read Introduction to Chapter 1 and John Updike, "On Being a Self Forever." Dialectical Notebook Entry (left-hand side notes).

WEEK 2
Mon -- Group Work: Rhetorical Strategies
Large Group Discussion: Reflecting on the Reading and Rhetorical
Strategies
Homework: Informal Writing (2-3 pages)

Wed -- Sharing from Informal Writings and further discussion of Updike.
Homework: Read Iserhoff
Complete Dialectical Notebook entry (left-hand side notes)

Fri -- Group Work: Reflecting on the Reading
Large Group Discussion: Reflecting on the Reading and Rhetorical
Strategies
Homework: Informal Writing (2-3 pages)
Return to Dialectical Notebook Entries and complete right-hand side

WEEK 3
Mon -- Complete discussion of Iserhoff (if needed)
Discussion of Global, Organizational and Polishing Revision. Mini-
workshop on organization at the paragraph and essay level.
Homework: Begin Coles's "Entitlement"

Wed -- Model Peer Critique workshop
Homework: Finish Coles (Complete Dialectical Notebook entry)

Fri -- Group work: Rhetorical Strategies
Large Group Discussion on Rhetorical Strategies and Reflecting on the
Reading
Homework: Read "Ruth's Song"
Begin draft of paper #1, Sequence 2 or 3 (your choice)

WEEK 4
Mon -- Large Group Discussion on "Ruth's Song"
Group work for end of chapter sequence 2 or 3 (If working on 2, replace
"Killing Rage" and "Boys Will Be Men" with "On Being A Self Forever."
If working on 3, replace "Killing Rage" and "Boys Will Be Men" with
"Ruth's Song.")
10 minutes -- class writing on Reflecting on the Reading prompt
Homework: Finish draft and bring copies for peer critique

Wed -- peer critique workshops
Homework: Begin revising paper #1
Begin reading "An American of Color"
Begin Dialectical Notebook Entries

Fri -- Debrief from Peer Critiques
Preliminary discussion of "An American of Color"
Homework: Finish "An American of Color" and Dialectical Notebook
Entries
Finish revision of paper #1

WEEK 5
Mon -- Paper #1 due to teacher
Group Work: Understanding Rhetorical Strategies
Large Group Discussion on Rhetorical Strategies and Reflecting on the
Reading
In class informal writing: What can we learn from "An American of
Color" about learning and schooling in relationship to race and class?
Homework: Return to Dialectical Notebook Entries
Begin Reading Geertz "'From The Native's Point of View'"

Wed -- Preliminary discussion of Geertz
Community-based Groups: Brainstorming draft of your code of conduct
Homework: Finish Geertz and Dialectical Notebook Entries

Fri -- Large Group Discussion on Reflecting on the Reading (Geertz) and
Rhetorical Strategies

Consider: What do we learn from Geertz that will help us with our community partners?
Homework: Complete Dialectical Notebook and Entries
Draft of Paper #2 -- Sequence 8: Reflexivity from the Meta-sequences prompt #1 or #2, your choice

WEEK 6
Community-Based Project Begins This Week
Mon -- peer critique workshops on Paper #2
Homework: Read Introduction to Chapter 4
Begin revising Paper #2

Wed -- Discussion of Introduction to Chapter 4
Work in groups to refine Code of Conduct
Homework: Revise Paper #2

Fri -- Paper #2 due to instructor
Share Codes of Conduct and make final preparations to share these with your community partners
Homework: Write first triple-entry incident journal entry
Research as much as you can about your community partner in the library and on the Web. While in the library find two sources (article or books) that focus on the issues or subject you think your community partner works with. Bring to class.

REMEMBER: YOU ARE SCHEDULED TO MEET, AS A GROUP, WITH YOUR COMMUNITY PARTNER SOME TIME NEXT WEEK. TAKE YOUR CODE OF CONDUCT.

WEEK 7
Mon -- Meet in Community-based groups. Based on the sources you found in the library and on the Web, determine who will be responsible for reading which sources and supplying an oral summary back to the group.
Write second triple-entry incident journal entry
Homework: Begin reading and preparing oral summaries

Wed -- Group 1 (ABLE)   Group 2 (HeadStart)
Prepare a list of questions you have for your community partner regarding tutoring expectations and the background of their clients.

Group 3 (Educational Cooperative)
Prepare a list of questions regarding needs and expectations to take with you to your community partner meeting. Also, draw up a tentative outline for researching and completing the writing of the grant. Make sure you go over this very carefully with your community partner.
Homework: Continue reading and preparing oral summaries. Write third triple-entry incident journal after meeting with your client.

Fri -- Large group debriefing from meetings with clients. Groups: Finalize writing timelines.
Remember: Groups 1 and 2:
In the next seven weeks you must complete (including peer critique sessions) the following three projects: Social Analysis and Commentary; Reflective and Reflexive Narrative; and an Assessment of the Community-Based Project.
Group 3: In the next seven weeks you must have completed (including peer critique sessions): Your grant proposal for your community partner, a social analysis and commentary OR a Reflective and Reflexive Narrative, and an Assessment of the Community-Based Project.
All groups must also build in two more sets (three entries) of triple-entry incident journal responses.
Homework: Final preparations for Oral Summaries

WEEK 8
Mon -- Oral Summaries presented to groups

Wed -- Oral Summaries presented to groups

Fri -- Large class discussion of final questions and concerns before complete immersion in community-based projects.
In-class writing: Reflections on the course and the upcoming project.

WEEKS 9-15
Mondays and Wednesdays will be spent in planning sessions for writing projects, peer critique and review workshops, general check-ins with the large group, and handling of issues and problems as they arise.

We will not meet on Fridays with the entire class. This hour will go toward the five hours per week you will spend with your community partners.

FINALS WEEK: Final meeting time to be announced. All Community-Based Projects must be gathered into a collection for the final grade and are due at this final exam meeting.

Sample Syllabus Four: 15 weeks, 2 or 3 Times Weekly, Entirely Community-based (Oral History Project)

I. Preparing for the Project

Week One   Introduction: The idea of the course
              Reflective Prewriting: Write on one (or more) of the
                    prompts at the beginning of Chapter 4
              Class discussion

              What is Community-Based Writing?
                    Read Introduction, Chapter 4
              What is an Oral History Project?
                    Read "Oral History Projects: Introduction"
              Class discussion

              The Idea of Oral History
                    Read Terkel, "Working the Land"
                    Prior to class, freewrite on one of the Reflecting on
                          The Reading or Understanding Rhetorical
                          Strategies prompts at the end of this
                          selection

Class discussion

Week Two   Read Terry, "Private First Class Reginald 'Malik'
              Edwards"
              Prior to class, freewrite on one of the Reflecting on
                  The Reading or Understanding Rhetorical
                  Strategies prompts at the end of this
                  Selection
              Class discussion

              Read Tateishi, "Violet de Cristoforo–Tule Lake"
              Prior to class, freewrite on one of the Reflecting on the
                  Reading or Understanding Rhetorical Strategies
                  prompts at the end of this selection
              Class discussion

Week Three   Read Yow, "Varieties of Oral History Projects: Community
              Studies"
              Prior to class, freewrite on one of the Reflecting on the
                  Reading or Understanding Rhetorical Strategies
                  prompts at the end of this selection
              Class discussion

Note: At this point instructor might wish to give students a more or less traditional formal writing assignment, both to get them started writing and to provide them with an opportunity to think more deeply about the oral histories they have read. The instructor so inclined might draw either from the writing prompts following each selection or the prompts in End-of-Chapter Sequences #2 and #3. The latter, dealing with the form and the historical import of oral histories, respectively, are especially useful for sensitizing students to some of the nuances of the project they themselves are about to undertake.

Week Four   Selecting a Project
             Generate a list of communities or subcommunities within
                   which we might conduct an oral history project
                   (End-of-chapter Sequence #1, step #1)
             Select group, develop project goals statement (sequence #1,
                   step #2
             Who is our audience for this project?

             What do we know about this group?
                   In small groups: generate a list of what we know–
                   and don't know—about this group (sequence #1,
                   step #3).

             Preliminary research: Divide class in half
                   Group 1: Conduct research on the community
                         selected
                   Group 2: Conduct research on how to organize and
                         conduct an oral history project. (sequence
                         #1, step #4)

Week Five   Conduct informational interviews, identify potential
             narrators; that is, individuals to interview
                   (sequence #1, step #5)

             Develop an interview guide (sequence #1, step #6)

             Reports on Preliminary research
             Class discussion
             Expectations: Determine the number of interviews
                   expected of each student

II. Conducting the Interviews

Weeks Six through Eleven   Conduct and transcribe interviews
(sequence #1, project #2)

Students maintain triple-entry incident journal for each interview
(sequence #1, project #1)

Note: During this stage, class meets less frequently–say, once a week–so students will be expected to be responsible for the productive use of their time. Weekly class meetings will provide an opportunity for students to provide peer responses of their classmates' oral history transcripts-in-progress as well as their headnotes (sequence #1, project #3), and for instructor to monitor student progress. In addition, time should be allotted for a discussion of what's working, what's not working, and of problems, as necessary. Instructor should reserve the right to call additional class meetings or make adjustments in the schedule, as the situation warrants.

III. Putting It All Together

Week Twelve   Final peer reviewing, editing of oral histories, to include
determining where followup interviews are needed

Whole Class: Read all oral histories, decide how they
should be grouped, ordered

Brainstorm General Introduction for the collection
[Assumes class has decided to collect oral histories
into a single volume for publication in some form]
Determine who will write which parts of
Introduction, who will edit (sequence 1, project #4)

Week Thirteen   Whole Class: Review of Successive Drafts of
Introduction
Other editorial tasks as needed

Note: From here on out class can be conducted as a workshop. Students not directly involved in putting together the final publication should be drafting, peer reviewing, and revising the final writing assignments for the course. Here is a point at which peer response is especially productive, since it permits students engaged in reflecting upon their experience a number of opportunities to see how other students are making sense of theirs.

Draft #1, Assessment of the Project, due
    May be done individually or as a class
    (sequence #1, project #5)

Week Fourteen   Draft #2, Assessment of the Project, due

Draft #1, Reflective and Reflexive Narrative, due
    (sequence #1, project #6)

Week Fifteen   Draft #2, Reflective and Reflexive Narrative, due

Begin assembling Final Portfolio, drafting critical, reflective introduction

Finals Week   Final Portfolio due. Portfolio is a collection of all six of the previous writing projects, plus a critical, reflective introduction to your work, approximately 4-6 pages. (sequence #1, project #7)

Further Thoughts and Resources on
Community-based Learning and Service Learning

Engaging students in community-based learning and community service has been very exciting and rewarding work for us and for our students. It is often demanding and challenging to add community components to our writing courses, but it is one way to bring reflexivity, writing, and action together. We find no better way to immerse students in civic participation, in understanding the ways various cultures, institutions, agencies, communities, and individuals are shaped by language, and how they, as language users, can shape their own situations through rhetorical contexts.

In addition to the information and suggestions we make in the Introduction to Chapter 4 of *Writing As Reflective Action*, we wanted to share a list of resources that our own institutions provide to Ohio University and Portland State faculty interested in pursuing community-based learning or service learning. What follows is a profile of one service learning project, selected Internet and printed-text resources, lists of service learning projects at our universities, and a brief history of service learning at Ohio University. The profile and other examples are not necessarily writing courses, but they all could be adapted to the writing course.

Profile of an Ohio University Service
Learning Project: Reading Buddies

When I developed a new course, Transformational Leadership with Emotional Intelligence, it was important to the learning process for students to complete a community service learning project so that students could practice theories learned in class. It's one thing to think and talk about being emotionally intelligent as a leader—to actually be a leader brings the theories to life. (Dr. Mary Tucker)

The Service Learning Context: West Elementary is a Title I pre-kindergarten-sixth grade school located on the west side of town. Students come from a variety of socioeconomic backgrounds. Approximately 36% of the student population qualifies for free and reduced lunch. State test scores indicate that 59% of the fourth grade students are proficient in reading and math. This holds true of our sixth grade population.

The Community Partner Perspective: The College of Business at Ohio University and West Elementary have formed a partnership which provides one-on-one tutoring to about 70 of our elementary students, particularly in reading and math. Children who are at-risk for learning respond well to individual attention. Working one-on-one focuses students on their task and bolsters their self-esteem by placing them in a learning environment within which they are more likely to succeed. In addition, students feel valued knowing that there is yet another adult who cares about their well being. The OU students are true partners in the education of the students at West.

Ohio University Students' Responses to the Community Project

The Classroom Atmosphere:

For the past eight weeks I went to West Elementary School in Athens and worked with Miss Moore's first grade class. The first day that I went into the classroom I was very nervous. I have never worked with children before and I had no idea what to expect. To my surprise, the whole experience turned out to be a great one. Now, I feel much more comfortable in the classroom and around the children. The teacher, Miss Moore, was extremely nice and really appreciated it when I came in to help the children with their reading. After just a few weeks of visiting the classroom, I really started to get attached to the children. Every time I would walk into the room, the kids would all yell my name, run up to me and almost knock me down with a big hug. It felt good to know that the kids liked me and looked up to me. They would beg the teacher to let them be the first group to read with me for the day, and when it was time for me to go, I would get the same big hug that I was greeted with.

50

Sometimes, the teacher would even have to tell them to let go of me so I could leave.

Rewards from this Experience:

I found that the best part of working with children is their unconditional love for you. I forgot how trusting and innocent small children are. The children hardly even know me, yet they are always excited to see me and they can't wait to tell me all about themselves. It was so rewarding when the children wanted to be the first ones to read with you and they were so excited about the books that you were helping them with. The most difficult thing about working with the children was that I wish I had more time to spend with them and not just read with them. I really wished I could spend extra time with the children outside of the learning atmosphere. Many times the children wanted to talk to me and tell me about things that were going on in their lives, but since my purpose was to tutor them in reading, I had to stick to the schedule so they would get their assignments done.

Evaluation of What I Learned:

At first, I thought that it was odd that I would have to do community service as part of a management class. Now that I have completed the course and the service learning project I see that the two do overlap. When working with the children, you learn a lot about leading with emotional intelligence. Children pick up on everything, so anything you say and do will be remembered. It is also very important to pay close attention to the children so that you can react to their moods and feelings. One thing I learned about being a leader is that it really helps your followers when you use reinforcements. I found this was especially true with the children. You get the best results with encouragement. I assume that these types of tips would not only be handy in the classroom, but also in the business world. Not that you want to treat your employees like first graders, but the same concepts in leading children carry over to leading adults. This community service project also taught me a lot about the community. When you live in a college town, it is easy to forget about the residents around you who are not college students. By working with residents of the community, it makes you realize that you should be giving back to the town that you can call home for four years of your life instead of just taking from it. Working at the elementary school gives us, the students, an opportunity to do this.

Benefits:

There are many important benefits of integrating community service with academic classes. The most obvious benefit is to the children and community. By making community service part of the class curriculum, we were all forced to give it a try. Without this class I would have never realized how easy it was to volunteer and I probably would have never tried it. Just giving a little of your time can make a big difference, especially when it comes to working with children. By working with the children one-on-one I was able to give them the attention they need to learn to read faster. Not only does community service benefit the children, but it also benefits the volunteers. I learned a lot about working with children and people in general. I was involved in something I could really feel good about and I was proud to tell others about what I was doing. A community service such as this one is one that looks great on a resume and is a great conversation topic in a job interview. I think combining community service with academics is a great idea and Dr. Tucker really has come up with a great way of integrating the two.
--Ohio University Student

Selected Internet Resources

The following is a list of Internet homepage addresses of some national organizations that address literacy, education, service and service learning. With the growing availability of Internet access and the corresponding surge in the number of websites, we cannot provide a complete listing of relevant sites. These are the twenty sites Ohio University faculty have found to be most accessible. Many of them contain links to other related sites.

American Association for Higher Education (AAHE):
http://www.aahe.org

American Council on Education: http://ace-info-service.nche.edu/home.html

Campus Compact: http://www.compact.org

Campus Outreach Opportunity League (COOL):
http://www.COOL2SERVE.org

Chronicle of Higher Education:
http://chronicle.merit.edu/.guide/.eguide.html

Corporation for National Service (CNS): http://fdncenter.org

Language and Literacy Project:
http://www.uis.edu/~cook/langlit/index.html

Literacy and Education Archive: http://english-www.hss.cmu.edu/LVA

National Association of Service and Conservation Corps (NASCC):
http://www.nascc.org

National Center for the Study of Writing and Literacy:
http://www-gse.berkeley.edu/research/NCSWL/csw.homepage.html

National Institute for Literacy: http://novel.nifl.gov

National Education Services (NES): http://www.nes.org

National Service Learning Cooperative Clearinghouse:
http://www.nicsl.coled.umn.edu

National Service Resource Center: http://www.etr.org/NSRC

Service Learning Home Page: http://csf.colorado.edu/sl

Student Coalition for Action in Literacy Education (SCALE):
http://www.unc.edu/depts/scale

U.S. Department of Education: http://www.ed.gov

Youth Service America: http://servenet.org

Selected Printed Resources

The following is an additional short list of texts that Ohio University
teachers have found useful as they have added community-based learning
and service to their courses. As with the Internet sources, there have been
many publications on service learning, and we encourage you to look
beyond the list we have here.

"Assessing the Impact of Service Learning." Portland State University,
1998.

Eyler, Janet. *Where's the Learning in Service-Learning?* Jossey-Bass,
1999.

Eyler, Janet. *Practitioner's Guide to Reflection in Service-Learning.*
Vanderbilt University, 1996.

Ford, Marjorie and Ann Watters. *A Guide for Change: Resources for
Implementing Community Service Writing.* McGraw Hill, 1995

Jacoby, Barbara. *Service-Learning in Higher Education: Concepts &
Practices.* Jossey-Bass, 1996.

Redesigning Curricula: Models of Service Learning. Campus Compact,
Brown University, 1994.

Rhoads, Robert. *Academic Service Learning: A Pedagogy of Action and Reflection.* Jossey-Bass, 1998.

Zlotkowski, Ed. Editor. *Writing the Community: Concepts and Models for Service Learning in Composition.* AAHE Series on Service-Learning in the Disciplines, 1997.

Sample List of Service Learning and Community-Based Learning Projects: Ohio University, Athens Campus:

BA 470 - Business Policy and Strategy
David Chappell - Business Management Systems
Students create business or marketing strategies to be presented to a community-based organization client in this project-based course.

Dance 490 - Dance for Multiply Challenged Children
Marina Walchli - Dance
Students teach multiply challenged and developmentally disabled children employing theory and conceptual development of dance and creative movement.

EDCI 101 Democracy and Education
Jaylynne Hutchinson - Teacher Education, Athens
Students will volunteer twenty hours in a community agency during the quarter assisting with services and learning strategies for connecting the classroom to community.

EDCI 492 - Curriculum Development
Rosalie Romano - Teacher Education
Students will create expeditionary learning projects in public schools to explore topics of local cultural history such as coal mining, economic development and Appalachian life.

EDEL 350 - Methods of Teaching Social Studies
Ginger Weade - Teacher Education
As part of methods class student teachers will engage the elementary students in community service projects and facilitate structured reflection to integrate the service experiences with the social studies curriculum.

EDSP 670 - Technological Applications in Special Education
Scott Sparks - Teacher Education
Students provide service to an individual or agency that utilizes technology as part of their everyday life. Through this service they gain insight as to the effect of technology on society.

EDVE 360A - Observations/Visitations
Terry Harvey - Teacher Education
Practicing vocational teachers research service-learning pedagogy and how it can be integrated into high school vocational programs.

EDVE 360B - Observations/Visitations
Terry Harvey - Teacher Education
Practicing vocational teachers develop a video tape demonstrating a service-learning lesson and implement a project with high school vocational students.

EDVE 360C - Observations/Visitations
Terry Harvey - Teacher Education
Practicing vocational teachers evaluate service-learning activities carried out with their high school vocational students.

ENG 153 Freshman Writing - Special Projects
Jane Denbow - English
Students work with community-based organizations, providing research and writing for projects such as brochures, grant proposals, and training manuals.

ENG 305J - Technical Writing
Roy Flannagan - English
Students work with community-based organizations, providing research and writing for projects such as brochures, grant proposals, and training manuals.

GEOG 350 - Environmental Land Use Planning
Nancy Bain - Geography
Student groups develop land use planning proposals for several Athens city areas and neighborhood associations.

HCCF 260 - Diversity in Early Childhood Education
Cheryl Vanhook - Human and Consumer Science
Students will work with local early childhood education providers to enhance their services, 3-4 hours per week.

HCCF 371 - Family Development
Jenny Chabot - Human and Consumer Sciences
Students volunteer time to different local agencies offering services to families, while gaining an understanding of individual development in families as a lived experience.

HCCF 462/562 - Pluralistic Lifestyles
Karen Wilcox - Human and Consumer Sciences
Students work with community-based organizations providing services to children and families, and exploring cultural issues and service development.

HCRM 250 - The Consumer in American Society
Ann Paulins - Human and Consumer Sciences
Students engage in service to the community to better understand factors influencing economic and consumer freedom. They also study consumer advocacy groups.

HRM 420 - Introduction to Human Resource Management
Cedric Dawkins - Interpersonal Communications
Students will work on human resource management projects with local agencies. Issues such as training, recruiting, benefits and performance appraisal will provide research and planning opportunities for students and services for agencies.

HCRM 423 - Retail Promotional Strategies
Letty Workman - Human and Consumer Science
Students produce marketing plans for local clients while developing their own intellectual skills, examining legal and ethical strategies, problem solving, and team cohesion.

HLTH 413 - Health Aspects of Aging
Gari Lesnoff-Caravaglia - Health Sciences
Students work with members of the aging population to observe lifestyle, health and problems while providing support and assistance.

HSS 730 - Geriatric Communication Disorders
Brooke Hallowell - Hearing and Speech Sciences
Students work with systems of caregivers to enhance services, conduct training, and establish support services for caregivers.

INCO 405 - Meeting and Conference Planning
Roger Aden - Interpersonal Communication
Students work on projects with community-based organization clients to propose, develop, and plan conferences and meetings.

INCO 406 - Advanced Interpersonal Communication
Christina Beck - Interpersonal Communication
The class designs a workshop on conflict management for several hundred public school students in first through sixth grades.

INCO 530 - Communication and the Campaign
John Smith - Interpersonal Communication
Students work with local organizations or individuals in an effort to increase membership, raise funds, or to raise awareness about their services.

JOUR 331 - Reporting Contemporary Issues: Sports Writing
Sandra Haggerty - Journalism
Students help children enhance self-esteem by recognizing skills and accomplishments in playground games. Students then report on the activities in the local media.

JOUR 370 - Media Relations and Publicity Writing
Bojinka Bishop - Journalism
Students will work in teams to produce public relations information and materials for local organizations.

JOUR 450 - Qualitative Methods in Communications Research
Jeanne Steele - Journalism
Students work with local community-based organizations to identify research questions and design studies in response to these questions.

MGT 491 - Seminar: Creativity and Ideas for Business
Gary Coombs - Business Management
In conjunction with a graphics design class, student groups plan, design and create educational games for use by community-based organizations.

MGT 491 - Seminar: Transformational Leadership
Mary Tucker - Business Management
Students apply leadership and mentoring knowledge based on the study of emotional intelligence and other theories through acting as Reading Buddies at local elementary schools.

MKT 202 - Marketing Module
Ashok K. Gupta - Marketing
Working with local service organizations, students come to understand
how basic marketing ideas are applicable to businesses, particularly
community-based service organizations.

MKT 379/579 - Marketing Research
Elizabeth Blair - Marketing
Students carry out marketing research on the effects of smoking for the
Athens Health Department while at the same time developing their skills
in marketing research.

MKT 444 - Consumer Behavior
Jane Sojka - Marketing
Students work with Ohio University's Speech and Hearing Clinic to
develop a plan for communicating information about their services to their
target markets.

NBSP 490 - Independent Study
Sharon Denham - Nursing
Students conduct a needs assessment and write a proposal for providing
health services. Subsequent classes do health assessments, evaluation,
referrals and screenings.

OPIE 045 - American Experience
Gerry Krzic - Ohio Program of Intensive English, Athens
International students volunteer in local agencies in order to enhance their
understanding of American life, to share their knowledge and to practice
language skills.

POLS 540 - The Politics of Developing Areas
Lisa Aubrey - Political Science
Students engage in local community development activities and then tie
these experiences to larger issues in national and international
development.

REC 201 - Recreation for Individuals with Disabilities
Sheri Perkins - Recreation and Sport Science
Students work with community agencies to design and implement recreation activities for individuals with disabilities.

REC 250 - Recreation Leadership
Beth VanDerveer - Recreation and Sport Science
Students spend 12 to 15 hours working with an agency that provides recreation/leisure services helping them solve problems and complete tasks.

SW 190 - Social Work as a Profession
Karen Slovak - Social Work
Students spend twenty-five hours volunteering at a community social services agency. From the experience they gain insight to the social work profession as well as gain volunteer field experience.

SW 380 - Abuse and Neglect
Carolyn Tice - Social Work
Students conduct direct and indirect service to community-based organizations serving populations faced with issues of abuse and neglect.

SW 382 - Understanding Alcohol Problems & Alcoholism
Karen Townsend Carlson - Social Work, Athens
Students will provide services to community agencies dealing with alcoholism issues, 10-12 hours per week.

TCOM 318 - Video Production II
Sheila Wurtsbaugh - Telecommunications
Students work with organizations developing a video program for promotion of the subject or education of the community.

TCOM 319 - Video Production III
Roger Good - Telecommunications
Students produce a documentary video that will support grant proposals
and serve as recruitment and publicity programming for a homeless
shelter.

TCOM 331 - Broadcast Writing
Sandra Sleight-Brennan - Telecommunications
Students design a public service announcement campaign, writing radio
and television spots for the client.

TCOM 869R - Action Research
William Miller - Telecommunications
Students serve as change agents in the areas of team building,
organizational structure and communication for a community group or
organization.

Tier III 463A- Theatrical Space & Performance
Bill Condee - Theater
Students engage local rural communities in plans to develop programming
for and restoration of historical opera houses.

 UC 125 - Freshman Seminar
Ted Bernard- Geography
Students work with a local community-based organization. They use and
further develop critical thinking and analytical skills in providing service
of an environmental nature.

Sample List of Service Learning and Community-Based Learning Projects, Portland State University[*]

ANTH 415 – Applied Anthropology
Margaret Everett – Anthropology
Upper-division undergraduate and graduate students used applied methods of anthropology in research conducted for a variety of organizations.

LING 478/578 – TESOL Methods II
Marjorie Terdal – Applied Linguistics
Thirty-two undergraduate students taught English as a Second Language (ESL) to refugees and immigrants from Vietnam, Mexico, Russia, Eastern Europe, Africa and Korea. Many focused on citizenship (passing the test) and survival skills.

ARCH 460, 461,462 – Architect Design Studio III
L. Rudolph Barton – Architecture
Students worked on architectural/urban design issues with the City of Gresham. Their projects involved an examination of the defined edge of the city as it borders Portland, "mixed use" opportunities within a ten-block area to be revitalized, and design issues around transportation.

ART 321 – Graphic Design II
Susan Agre-Kippenhan – Art
Thirty PSU undergraduates designed logos, letterheads, and public relations material for Friends of the Children, the Three Valleys Projects, and the Multnomah Commission on Aging.
BIO 471 – Plant Ecology

Bob Tinnin – Biology
PSU Students conducted ecological evaluations of Beacon Hill Park and Lowami Nature Park in partnership with the Tualatin Hills Park and Recreation District.

---

[*] For this information, we are indebted to "Community-University Partnerships at Portland State University, 1995-2000."

BST 399, 410, 409 – Caribbean Overseas Program
Candice Goucher – Black Studies
PSU Undergraduate students designed and taped a community program on the changing roles of Caribbean women.

BA 399 – Interview Training
Talya N. Bauer – Business Administration
Students provided interview training and resume assistance to 12 adolescents in the Nightscape program sponsored by the Schnitzer Foundation.

CFS 407 – Interdisciplinary Perspectives on Children and Families
Lola Lawson – Child and Family Studies
Thirty PSU undergraduate students worked with children and families on cultural conflicts, issues, and goals in community placements.

CS 409 – Computer Science Practicum
Warren Harrison – Computer Science
Students worked in the "Software Testing Laboratory" testing software products for local companies.

CAPS 410/510 – Program Evaluation in a Nonprofit Social Service Agency
Conrad Sieber – Counseling and Psychological Services
Twenty undergraduate and graduate students devised a program evaluation plan for the Dougy Center as well as conducted telephone surveys, literature reviews, updated the Dougy Center library, and gathered information about the program.

CI 406/506 or EPFA 406/50 – Service Delivery for Youth
Samuel Henry – Education
Eight undergraduate students developed reports describing Multnomah County resource centers at various schools. These reports were written for various integrated service centers (in conjunction with the Multnomah County Commission on Children and Families).

ENG 308 – Immigrant Experience and American Literature and Film
Sue Danielson – English
Fifty-five PSU undergraduate students were paired with ENNR (English for Non-native Residents) students and adults from Portland Public Schools for tutoring/mentoring. The PSU students printed oral histories of recent immigrants, assisted staff at SOAR (Sponsors Organized to Assist Refugees) with Somalian refugees, and assisted with the moving process for new immigrants.

ENVS 203 – Applied Environmental Studies Project
James R. Pratt – Environmental Sciences and Resources
Undergraduate students provided initial instruction in field analysis methods in environmental science followed by application of sampling techniques to the analysis of real problems in the community.

FL 405/505 – Internship: Mentoring/Tutoring Russian Students in Portland Public Schools
Lida O'Donnell, Martha Hickey – Foreign Languages and Literatures
Students tutored and mentored recent refugees (students) in Marshall and Jefferson high schools in the English language and U. S. Culture.

HST 316 – American Family History
David Johnson – History
Thirty-five PSU undergraduate students developed family histories for senior citizens living in subsidized housing in the University neighborhood.

ASC 201 – Modeling Nature and Life
Gerardo Lafferriere – Mathematical Sciences
Students worked with the HIV Day Center and Ecumenical Ministries of Oregon using mathematical modeling to schedule delivery of hot meals to locations in the metro area.

MUS 409 – Piano Teacher Training Program
Mary Hall Kogen – Music
PSU students provided music lessons for students at Self-Enhancement Incorporated and the Pacific Crest Community School.

PSY 480, 481, 482; 580, 581, 582; or US 407/507 – Community Psychology
Hugo Maynard – Psychology
Undergraduate and graduate students participated in a variety of projects: developing and administering surveys to various community organizations; serving as a liaison between high school staff and students with special needs; mentoring problem students; training student mediators in schools for non-violent resolution of disputes among students; mentoring ESL high school students and students in YMCA school for children of homeless families.

PA 510 – Managing Boards and Commissions
Suzanne Feeney – Public Administration
Twenty-five graduate students conducted interviews and assessments for reflection on relationship of theory to practice and leadership theory to special needs and characteristics of nonprofits in the community.

PHE 410 – Environmental Health
Phil Kreitner – Public Health Education
Students worked in teams to study local hospital materials management system to determine the nature of their bio-hazardous waste handling system and the potential for reduced production and safer disposal.

SOC/USP 399 – Social Psychology of Recycling
Peter Collier – Sociology
Fifteen PSU undergraduate students taught a recycling awareness program at Grant and Roosevelt high schools to promote involvement of high school youth in recycling and waste reduction issues in their schools and local neighborhoods. The high school students developed and conducted similar programs for Clarendon and Irvington elementary schools.

SP 399 – Intergenerational Communications
Janelle Voegele – Speech Communication
Undergraduate students mentored elderly patients at the Robinson Jewish Home in the creation of "memory books."

SPHR 586 – Urban Language Clinic
Ellen Reuler – Speech and Hearing Sciences
Graduate students provide enrichment in speech and language development in a classroom setting to children who are homeless.

UNST 299 – Classic Greek Civilization, Sophomore Inquiry
Karen Eva Carr – University Studies
Students in this Sophomore Inquiry class created and maintain a World Wide Web site about Greek civilization for the benefit of middle school and elementary school students across the country. The site has been heavily used by students and teachers across the country, averaging about 1,500 "hits" each month.

USP 410/510 and PSY 410/51 – Doing Focus Group Research
David Morgan – Urban Studies and Planning
Twenty-four undergraduate and graduate students conducted focus group research to assist the PSU Bookstore in assessing customer satisfaction.

A Brief History of Service Learning at Ohio University[*]

Following is a chronology of activities intended to advance Ohio University's adoption of service-learning that have been undertaken by the partnership of the Center for Community Service and University College. Prior to and throughout the time period represented, individual faculty and departments have incorporated service learning into courses, curricula and programs.

---

[*] Our thanks to Merle Graybill, Director, Center for Community Service at Ohio University, for providing this history.

1992

- In summer 1992, a faculty/staff team attended the week-long seminar symposium on Integrating Service with Academic Study at Brown University.
- The former Ohio University Volunteer Center was redefined as the Center for Community Service.

1993

- The Brown team developed a discussion document on the topic "Educating for Citizenship"; distributed to chairs, directors, and selected faculty in March 1993.
- In April 1993, a day-long symposium on Integrating Service with Academic Study was hosted by OU and attracted faculty from around Ohio. This was funded by a grant from Ohio Campus Compact and the Corporation for National Service. Keynoters were Dr. Ben Barber and Dr. Gary Hesser.
- In summer 1993, the Ohio University 1804 Fund allocated $82,650 to initiate a service-learning program on campus.
- A part-time administrative coordinator and a part-time faculty coordinator were hired.

1994

- An external grant was obtained by the Center in the amount of $9,000 (through the federal Serve America program) to support a demonstration service-learning project, the Junior Glouster Project. The project allowed staff the opportunity to work through an actual project and use the insights and information gained to help plan faculty development and administrative support efforts.
- An external grant in the amount of $3,000 was obtained by the Center (from the Corporation for National Service) to supplement the funds allocated by the 1804 Fund for the initiation of service-learning activities at OU.
- The administrative coordinator conducted site visits with more than 50 agencies and organizations in the Athens community for the purpose

of assessing service needs, receptivity to service-learning placements, and suitability for service-learning placements.

- The faculty coordinator identified an initial pool of over 20 faculty who had some level of interest in service learning. An assessment of needs was conducted during the fall of 1994. Faculty identified five particular needs: assistance in orienting students to service-learning, clarification of the institution's risk management strategy and the implications for faculty liability, assistance in brokering relationships with community-based organizations, assistance in student transportation, and on-going access to resource materials.

- A week-long institute devoted to service-learning course revision was developed by the faculty coordinator. A resource manual was developed. Faculty on Athens and regional campuses were invited to submit proposals for participation in the institute. Over 30 complete proposals were forwarded, though funding was available to support only 12 faculty. Additional funds were secured to allow a total of 17 faculty to participate.

- The week-long seminar was held in early December of 1994. All invited faculty attended. The seminar included sessions on designing and redesigning courses, agency-student-faculty relations, Appalachian culture, evaluating student performance, and trends/issues in service learning. Keynote speaker was Dr. Ed Zlatkowski.

- The Center for Community Service established a partnership with Rural Action, Inc. The partnership uses the resources of AmeriCorps VISTA (two full time VISTAs work at the Center) to develop a volunteer mobilization infrastructure that will assist both university and community volunteers in making connections and using a collaborative model; this infrastructure then also serves as a key resource for faculty engaged in service-learning.

1995
- The first of the revised courses were taught during winter and spring of 1995. Assistance was provided to faculty in obtaining placements/ referrals for students and in developing relationships with particular community-based organizations.

69

- A Faculty Advisory Board (FAB) was developed and meets quarterly. It includes nine faculty from five colleges.
- The Faculty Service-Learning Network (FSLN) was formed and meets quarterly. Its purposes are to provide for ongoing faculty development, to allow information/resources. Its current membership is 110. Average attendance at network meetings is 20.
- Assistance was provided to the College of Osteopathic Medicine and the Communication and Development Studies Program in preparing grant proposals to integrate service learning at a program level. OU-COM has since been awarded a grant of $32,486 from Pew Charitable Trusts (HPSISN).
- A group of seven faculty, students, and staff attended the Ohio Campus Compact Symposium on Service-Learning and presented two programs.
- A second service-learning seminar was held in November of 1995. Funding was provided by the deans of each of the colleges (to support his/her faculty participants). Ten faculty participated. Keynote speaker was Dr. Sharon Rubin.

1996

- In winter of 1996 the Center collaborated with Rural Action and faculty in the geography department in a SEAMS grant to connect GEOG 447/547 with the Monday Creek Restoration Project. A grant of $2775 was awarded for this purpose; course development was accomplished in spring of 1996 and the revised course was taught in fall of 1996.
- An evaluation of courses developed in the first year of the service-learning grant was completed, indicating that 13 courses (of 14 funded) had been taught; they involved 317 students who provided 8800 hours of service through more than 20 community-based organizations.
- The Faculty Advisory Board undertook the development of a set of criteria to be used in labeling service-learning courses. The board's recommendations were forwarded to Faculty Senate for its consideration in the fall of 1996.

- The third service-learning institute was held in December of 1996. Funding was provided by the deans of each of the colleges (to support his/her faculty participants). Ten faculty participated. For the first time the institute included a day-long service project (at Reuse Industries), followed by structured reflection. A growing proportion of training is presented by OU faculty. Dr. Dwight Giles was the keynote speaker.
- Four faculty members presented programs on service-learning at the following conferences: Ohio Campus Compact, Speech Communication Association, Association of Allied Health Professionals and Organizational Behavior Teaching.
- Ohio University President Robert Glidden convened two task forces on community and economic development and the quality of the University experience, respectively. Conclusions reached included decisions to encourage the integration of service with teaching and research as a component of a broader strategy aimed at improving the contribution of the University to the community and economic development of the region—and, in order to improve student experience, to support the integration of service learning in the curriculum.

1997
- Evaluation of year two courses was completed, indicating that 8 new courses were taught, involving 132 students in providing 3700 hours of service to 14 community-based organizations.
- Regional SEAMS Faculty Symposium was held at Ohio University in May of 1997 (funded by Ohio Campus Compact). It attracted 10 faculty in science, engineering, architecture, math and computer science from southeast Ohio.
- Learn & Serve Ohio University program proposal was funded by the Corporation for National Service for $115,000. A collaborative effort of the Center for Community Service, University College, the College of Education, and Rural Action, Inc., it supported five program activities designed to further the integration of service-learning on campus.

71

- Ohio University, through ILGARD, establishes a partnership with Hocking College to pursue cooperative service-learning activities between two- and four-year institutions through a program funded by the Corporation for National Service.
- President Glidden appoints five groups of faculty, students, and staff to continue the Pew Roundtable discussions. One of the groups, chaired by Dean Barbara Chapman with assistance of Gary Hunt, focused its discussion on connecting the university with community by integrating service and learning.

1998

- Full-time program coordinator was hired to carry out the activities of the Learn & Serve grant, which enabled the next steps in development of service learning at OU in five major respects:
  - Infusion of service-learning pedagogy into the curriculum of an academic unit, the College of Education and its teacher education, counselor education and higher education programs;
  - Collaboration with community-based organizations via a training for non-profit personnel in the principles of service-learning resulting in new partnerships between the university and the community, and the Learning Circle, and ongoing discussion of faculty, community and students about the practice of service-learning;
  - Research on the learning outcomes of service-learning carried out by faculty fellows;
  - Continued expansion of the number and quality of service-learning courses campus-wide;
  - Use of Federal Work Study funds to support students working in leadership roles in community service and service-learning.

Student Samples

Writing As Reflective Action is a demanding text, asking students to read, write, and think rhetorically. It asks students to understand and consciously engage in reflection and reflexivity, to think and write critically, to be willing to engage at a personal, academic, and civic level in ways few first-year students (and sometimes upper-division students) have been asked to do in their previous schooling. An amazing number of students rise to these challenges, some very successfully. Others, of course, struggle and their writing and thinking may remain less than we might have hoped. Nonetheless, the students who have worked through WRA with us have risen to the challenge as best they can, actively working toward reflection, reflexivity, rhetorical understanding, critical thinking, and civic participation through reading writing, and thinking, and, finally, toward writing for thinking and writing for expressing knowledge(s) they currently hold.

Both the examples from student informal writing and formal writing that follow show a range of student ability and success. They are included here because these students gave permission to use their writing. All, however, illustrate students grappling with reflexivity and trying to examine their subjects critically.

Informal Writing---Reading Response Journals

(Remember that in the informal writing neither the students nor the teachers are preoccupied with spelling, grammar, and mechanics. We have left the students' writing as they wrote it, then.)

Student Sample One:

Annie Iserhoff--"Excerpts From My Life" Reflecting on the Reading, Bullet #2: What are the major experiences Iserhoff has while growing up that lead her to changes or to seeing the world differently? Do you find yourself surprised at Iserhoff's responses to any of these experiences? Why or why not? Choose a specific passage to illustrate your thinking.

--Iserhoff has many different experiences while growing up which cause her to see the world differently. I think the first thing that happens to her to change her world is when her mother tells her that she cannot breast feed anymore. She feels unwanted and hurt by this, and it then starts her gradual detachment from her family. Another event is when she goes to the hospital. This long time away from home prepares her for the future, when she is forced to go to school. Even though she wants to go home, she is now used to being away from home. When she actually goes to school, she does not change very much, until she turns 14 and tells her father that she does not want to stay them, that she would rather go back to school. She starts to feel more and more independent from her family. After this, she starts to realize that people change and that she does not need her family as much as she used to. Once she does stay at home for an extended time, she realizes that it is not the same. She angers her family because she does not want to serve her little brothers. This completes her gradual independence from them.

I am not really too surprised by any of her responses. When she is little and has to leave her family, either to go to the hospital or to school, she cries, which is a normal response for any young child. When she is rejected by her family for not wanting to serve her little brother, she is upset and again cries. I think that anyone can relate to her passage "I gathered some stuff and ran out of the cabin...I felt like the world was against me...I cried for hours and hours at a time."

Student Sample Two:

What are the major experiences Iserhoff has while growing up that lead her to changes or to seeing the world differently? Do you find yourself surprised at Iserhoff's responses to any of these experiences? Why or why not? Choose a specific passage to illustrate your thinking.

--Iserhoff lived a very sheltered life until she was sent away to school. Because of her lifestyle, almost everything she experienced at school was new and many times hard for her. When one grows up in such a small, close-knit community, the ideas and actions of the world are hard to understand. For Iserhoff, understanding the actions of the teachers at her new school, doctors at the hospital, and those she met in life, were hard to figure out, which led to an even more isolated feeling. Growing up in a suburban community is much different than a small native village; however, I have also had experiences that changed my view of the world. In visiting Europe I saw that the whole world doesn't revolve around the United States and that not everyone sees it as the best country in the world. Living in such a large, dominant country for so long, one tends to miss the outside view. Fortunately for me I was given the chance to experience first, and not as tourist, the European way. This opened my eyes to many new and different opinions about life here. Like Iserhoff, I cam back to my home acting differently than when I left. When exposed to a new life it is hard to find a balance between the old and the new. I think Iserhoff had the same problem.

hooks, "Killing Rage"
bell hooks is writing about an anger that shakes her to the core, a "killing rage." What personal events does she tell us about that lead to this rage? What societal structures and events does she analyze for us?

--When I was a freshman in high school I played club soccer on one of the best teams in the state. Our club was known throughout the region and some teams in our club were well-respect throughout the country. Every time we went to a tournament many people came to watch our games, including college scouts. During the winter of my freshman year my team went to a very prestigious indoor tournament in Chicago. The best teams in the "Alliance" (a group of very good teams from the midwest and east that competed against each other in tournaments) were going to be present at this "Best in the Midwest Tournament". I had been working my butt off to get ready for this tournament because I knew many important coaches would be watching our games, as usual. We easily got through our round-robin bracket and were slotted to play the Illinois State champs in the semi-finals. When game time came I was pumped. My friend Jenny and I, played forward. Not to sound conceited, but we were the two best players on the team. Of 20 goals the team had scored in our previous 4 games in the tournament, 19 of them were scored by us. Indoor soccer is different than outdoors, in that the forwards don't just play up top. They come back on defense when necessary. Also, indoor soccer a player doesn't play the whole game, like in outdoors. However, Jenny and I played almost the whole semi-final game. We were up and down the field working our asses off. We were winning the game 2-1 with about 5 minutes left in the game. I was up near their goal and I lost the ball. Our team had many chances to stop the other team, but we didn't they scored and tied up the game. I blamed myself, which was wrong because I was on the other side of the field from the goal and we had a defense for that very reason, because your team loses the ball sometimes. Still, I was a mess. I thought I caused the goal and it was my fault we were in overtime. Overtime came and went and we were still tied. Time for penalty shots. I was an obvious choice for a PK. I had a great shot, I was the leading scorer on the team, and I was a captain. However, my coach thought I was too upset to concentrate on the shot, so he didn't pick me for the first five shooters. I was so upset, if I wasn't crying before I was after he told me I wasn't shooting. It wasn't a sobbing cry, but one of those crys where you are so mad you can barely talk. I felt I had let my team down and this was the one way I knew I could make it up. I yelled at my coach, but the more I yelled the harder I cried, leading my coach to believe I definitely was not stable enough to take a kick. I probably would have calmed down if he hadn't picked Amy for the 6th shot. She was the one person on the team I couldn't stand. She wanted my position so she went out of her to embarrass me or make me look bad on the field or in practice. Her parents were the same way. So over the course of 2 years on this team I had come to hate her. And now she was taking the final shot, the winning shot, when it should have been me. Well Amy go up to the line and tried to be fancy and do some fancy shot she had seen Jenny and I working on. She missed. We lost. Eliminated from a tournament we were supposed to in. In front of 30 college scouts I hadn't even taken a PK. I could have killed Amy at that moment. Who the hell did she think she was trying to be a star when all she had to do was shoot the ball. This wasn't the time nor the place to be trying a shot she would never be able to get. It took my coach, Jenny, my mom, my best friend from another team, and two other players to hold me back from socking her one. Needless to say she didn't come back to the team in the spring, because she "couldn't play for a captain who wanted to kill her." What incited my rage was different than Hooks, but the feeling of anger was the same. And once the feeling starts it really doesn't matter how it started.

Middleton, "Boys Will Be Men: Boys' Superhero Comics"
Identify, if you can, a favorite comic book or cartoon character. Write about why you are attracted to this character. Also write about what you think it says about you that you like this character.

--I have always liked Wonder Woman. I have gone as Wonder Woman for Halloween many times. When I was young someone told me I looked like her and I think that is how I became attached to her. I liked her ability to do anything. I have always been a very active person and I always like to be in charge. I think Wonder Woman's sense of power appealed to me. I like power. I seek power in most situations I come into. I think that is why I "relate" to her (as much as any human can relate to a comic!) That, and I can look like her.

Student Sample Three:

Iserhoff describes several ways in which her cultural background as a Native Indian living in Canada clashed with other cultures. What are some of the "clashes" she experienced? What seem to be the specific causes of these clashes? Can you identify some of the differing cultural assumptions that produced them?

--Iserhoff, from the beginning of the passage, indicates that her childhood was one of much pain. She explained that while most poeple have fond memories of childhood, her youth included more frightening and sad memories. As she tells her story it seems as if though she has left all this pain far behind her in her new life. The road to this life was very painful,

77

however. Much of her story is about leaving here home and her culture behind as well as not being able to fit into the french-canadian culture in front of her. She seemed to struggle with finding her sense of belonging and she may have never found it if it weren't for special people and circumstances along the way. I would say that by the end of her youth Iserhoff had left her native identity as well as the french identity behind and she had gained an identity of her own.

hooks, "Killing Rage"
hooks writes, "Confronting my rage, witnessing the way it moved me to grow and change, I understood intimately that it had the potential not only to destroy but also to construct." Read this sentence as a blueprint of hooks's essay itself and examine how her rage moves her to change and grow within the essay.

--When I first began reading "Killing Rage" it frightened me that it might be an essay based on rage. A writing with the full intention to vent anger built up against the world's ways. It happened to be just that. However, as I read through the pages I realized that the author had built up a rage within me, the reader. I almost couldn't take the notion that rage, especially a killing rage was acceptable and justified as the writer seemed to be implying. This idea was more acceptable when bell hooks wrote the paragraph starting with "Confronting my rage, witnessing the way it moved me to grow and change, I understood intimately that it had the potential not only to destroy but also to construct." The rest of the paragraph explained how the energy behind rage could be harnessed and put to a more positive use. I then understood that the point was not to inspire blind anger but to encourage minorities to think and analize their hate. Instead of acting on this energy wrongly or repressing it, bell hooks insisted that this rage be used to fight the prejudice in the world.

Middleton, "Boys Will Be Men: Boys' Superhero Comics"
Identify, if you can, a favorite comic book or cartoon character. Write about why you are attracted to this character. Also write about what you think it says about you that you like this character.

--As a child of eight or nine years old I can remember reading through my Spiderman comics over and over again. I had scanned the pictures of Spiderman battling the Hobgobin on building tops nearly a thousand times. I think the main thing that dew me to Spiderman was the fact that he actually ran the risk of dying or falling from great heights unlike the more prominent Superman and other flying heroes. Perhaps this was because I found it more masculine to face common fears. Superman had his vast super powers to rely on while Spiderman was armed only with his spider sense and his web shooting inventions. I was quite I paranoid child, therefore, a keen intuition such as spider sense was very intriguing to me. Meddleton might say that as a fearless man. Another thing that drew me to Spiderman was the fact that his true identity, Peter Parker, had been a high school nerd until a freak science experiment gave him his powers. The fact that he was a nerd in his day to day life gave him more credibility and allowed me to slip into Spiderman's shoes more easily. It wasn't nearly as long as a shot as Superman and it showed that I wouldn't need as many superpowers to prove my masculinity. As a daydreaming child I felt that there was a possibility that one day I could be Spiderman.

Formal Writing Samples

Student Sample One:

Chapter One End-of-Chapter Sequences
Sequence Three: Stories
"On Being a Self Forever"
"Excerpts From My Life"
"Killing Rage"
"Boys Will Be Men: Boys' Superhero Comics"

Writing Prompt #1: Write an essay in which you illustrate a point using personal stories of your own. This will be a stronger essay if you work with points of significant realization or change in your life. If you are a risk-taker, work with experiences or parts of your life that you do not yet fully understand.

Look at What We Have, as Americans

Throughout one's life, certain experiences, both good and bad can have a profound effect on the way one views or reflects upon his or her life. These experiences can change a persons feelings on certain issues and greatly affect a persons lifestyle. Although these experiences are not always positive ones, they still have the capability of great change in a person's life and how they view others. I had one such experience the summer before my junior year in high school that greatly affected my views on life. This experience was a trip overseas to the country of Belarus in the former Soviet Union. Belarus is located directly above the Ukraine and is a nation plagued with poverty and fatal illness.

It started in high school where I learned about Carpenters Tools, an organization that puts together several different groups of musicians and sends them overseas to raise money for another non-for-profit organization. I decided to audition. I recorded a ten-minute demo tape and send it to Minnesota where it was evaluated and critiqued. Later that month I received a call from the organization and they told me that I had made it and I would be traveling to Belarus for the summer. I was ecstatic to say the least. I had never been out of the country before and I knew that this was an opportunity of a lifetime; one that I could not pass up.

I began practicing and studying a select group of songs that would be on the set list at the concerts. This took a lot of time, about two months in fact, of practicing on my own. Later I had to travel Minnesota to meet up with my group and rehearse together. This is itself was a great experience. Living and practicing with a wide variety of people from all over the country was something that I won't soon forget. We were together twenty-four hours a day seven days a week. We had our arguments and misunderstandings but we all soon realized we had another three months to go, so we had better learn to get along. And we did. Everyone would have had a terrible experience if we never learned to put our differences behind us and move toward the future. This later proved to be very beneficial to the seven of us.

About two weeks later it was time to take off for Belarus. I had no idea what to look forward to and held little expectations. I knew very little about the country itself and even less about the people that I would encounter on this journey. After a series of flights throughout the United States with stops in Chicago and New York, we arrived in Warsaw, Poland. The seven of us were to stay in Warsaw for two days where we would take another flight to our final destination Minsk, Belarus. Stepping off the plane in Minsk I began to realize how fortunate I was to be an American citizen. The airport in Minsk was a small, dilapidated airport that didn't appear to be in very good condition. Everyone was a little shocked after viewing the condition of the airport but we were in fact on the ground and safe.

The next few days were the most difficult because of "culture shock" and the fact that I was forced into another place that was not home. It is a totally different way of life in Minsk and things are done much differently. Aside from differences in food and speech there are several differences in their culture. First and foremost Americans are much more rude and inconsiderate than the Belarussians. We as Americans tend to look at foreign visitors and be racist toward them. Americans even go as far as to ignore them as if they do not exist. The seven of us were treated like royalty. We were waited on hand and foot our entire stay. Older women would invite us to their homes for dinner and of course we would attend. I have never seen so much food in one place at one sitting. The kitchen table would be overflowing with food ranging from pancakes to borsch (cabbage soup), and the women would work all day preparing this meal. I have never experienced anything quite like it. It puts American family reunions to shame. The Belarussians are not the richest of people; in fact much of the country is poverty-stricken. Looking out of my hotel window I could see a family's home. It appeared to me to be a small shack or maybe storage shed. The wood on the outside of the house was old and rotting away. I could see all of the different colors that the wood had been painted previously; red, blue, brown and green were only some of the colors. The roof was made out of sheet of medal and was caving in the center. There were a variety of clothes hanging on the clothesline on the side of the house. This made me realize that there as a family of five or

81

six people living in this shanty. There was no grass around the house only a sea of brown dirt, which a little boy was playing in at the time. I can only imagine how much the families had to sacrifice to provide this meal that we by no means deserved.

This is only one example of how Belarussian values had a great impact on my life. This made me look at the world a little differently and realize that Americans are extremely selfish compared to people in other parts of the world. Another lesson that I learned about is gratefulness. Americans as a whole are very ungrateful people. I truly believe that it has something to do with our culture. Americans are so concerned with money and work that we don't have the time to think. We have so much to be thankful for but don't take the time out of our schedules to sit back and observe the things around us. Not only material items, such as computers, food and clothing, but also our land and natural resources.

Belarus, as I soon realized, is a very dirty country. Sanitation and cleanliness in the part of the world is a growing problem due mainly to problems with waste removal and water purifying systems. Looking out the window of the same hotel that we were staying in at the time I could see trash laying all over the alley. There were numerous piles of garbage and the majority of this garbage was not bagged. Trash was constantly blowing all over this alley. There were newspapers, rotting meat and boxes everywhere. The Belarrusian government is supposedly working to find a cure for this problem and trying to eliminate the spread of disease caused by the unsanitary conditions. Overall Americans need to take the time to sit back and realize how fortunate we as citizens really are.

As mentioned previously, Belarus is located directly above the Ukraine. At the border between Belarus and the Ukraine was a nuclear power plant. Chernobyl experienced a "meltdown" in the 1980's and radiation spread for hundreds of miles affecting much of the former Soviet Union. Water was contaminated along with the soil causing the radiation to spread rapidly and be passed down from generation to generation. I cannot tell you how many children I met that had some form of cancer or birth defect. Most of these birth defects would not be seen from the outside of the body but were destroying the kids on the inside. Some of these birth defects however could be seen from the outside. Some of these kids had brown spots or patches on their face and on their limbs. An individual patch looked like a birthmark but when combined with several others they looked like spots on a cow. These kids were extremely kind and warm-hearted people even though they knew that they did not have more than ten years to live. They are very curious about Americans and wanted to know everything about us. Where do you work? What are American schools like? What is your favorite food? These are some of the questions, that with the help of translators, we were able to communicate with them about and teach them some English at the same time. I later found out that the majority of these children would die before reaching the age of twenty-one. It was heart wrenching when I found out that these kids would never get a chance to experience children or a family of their own. It was a really sad moment in my life and still haunts me every time I think about it.

This experience with out a doubt changed my life. It made me realize several things about myself and others that I did not know before traveling overseas. For starters, I learned not to hold grudges or concentrate on the past. I now look toward the future and realize that arguments and disagreements only have to be a thing of the past. Another aspect of my life that I feel changed is the fact that I am much more grateful for what I have than what I was before. Americans as a whole are extremely selfish people and need to realize that what we, as Americans, have so much more then other countries. We have public schooling, healthcare and unlimited opportunities to do with out lives what we want. Much of the world is plagued by poverty, unsanitary conditions and the lack of a well-grounded government. We, as Americans need to take the time out of our busy schedules and look around us. Look at what we have. We shouldn't think about what we want that we do not have, but rather look at what we have and be thankful for it. We are living in the world of opportunity and many of us don't even realize it.

Student Sample Two:

Meta-Sequence Four: Private Experience as Public Argument
"Killing Rage"
"Ruth's Song"
"The Brass Ring and the Deep Blue Sea"
"On Being a Self Forever"
from *My Brother*
"Violet De Cristoforo--Tule Lake"
"Private First Class Reginald 'Malik' Edwards, Phoenix, Louisiana"

Writing Prompt #1: Choose two to four readings from the above list. Write an analysis of the argument being made in each essay. In other words, what is the argument? How and what evidence is the writer using? How does this argument work? And so on. Include clear discussions about the part that private experience is playing within the arguments.

I have two favorite readings from Writing as a Reflective Action, by Gradin and Carter. "Killing Rage" by bell hooks and "Private First Class" by Wallace Terry. These writings caught my fancy not because of what they said, but rather how it was presented. "Killing Rage" as far as content is not something that I would read. hooks, however, presents her work in such a way that I am compelled to read further. Wallace Terry functions in much the same way for me. Both writers have made me open my eyes wider in response to the sharing of their personal experiences.

"Killing Rage" by bell hooks is a story of racial injustice. As a black woman bell hooks is faced with issues of inequality every day. Her plight is not one concerning life and death circumstances of injustice. She faces small injustices every day. Small injustices not in significance but in +how we view them. I have read the story many times, and my attitude has changed significantly each time.

The first time I read "Killing Rage" I was angry. Her introduction made me want to read no further. It starts with this woman writing this essay sitting beside a anonymous male "that I [she] long to murder." As I read this I found myself very defensive. I immediately stopped listening. I was not willing to look at things from her point of view. I was only reading to fulfill my reading assignment.

On my second and subsequent readings of "Killing Rage," I began to see things from hooks' point of view. I did not necessarily agree with everything that she was saying but I listened. I began to understand why she felt as she did. She did not really want to kill the man in the beginning, she wanted to kill the injustice.

bell hooks writes to point out the problems with our way of life. She means to show us how we do not live in a perfect world. bell hooks does not want us to be complacent with our way of life. hooks encourages us to take the emotion that is developed in injustice and channel it into a positive venue that will facilitate change.

In Wallace Terry's story "Private First Class, Reginald 'Malik' Edwards" the subject of the oral history tells a tale of one man's war in Vietnam. Malik is a black marine who is part of a recon unit. Malik is a normal man in a war. Malik encounters many different situations in Vietnam. He is confronted by many situations which test him physically, emotionally, and morally.

Malik is in a war that he doesn't mind fighting because he is a American, and it is his duty to protect America. Malik thinks of himself as a warrior, he is a very capable marksman. At one point in the story he shoots the head off of a snake. The snake was not an immediate danger to him but Malik had no problem with shooting it. Only a few moments later he is in a situation in which he is confronted by the enemy. He shoots but misses. "All of the sudden I missed this old man. 'Cause I really couldn't shoot him." Malik has a inner struggle in which on one hand he wants to protect America and kill the enemy. But on the other hand he just does not want to take a life. When he does kill, it is not something which he has time to think about. A Vietnamese was charging his position with a gernade at night. Malik was faced with a action he didn't even think about, he killed. He didn't even think of the "gook" as a human, until after he was dead.

85

After he had killed the "gook" he was very excited and almost proud of his trophy. Then it hit him, the "gook" was a person with a family, and that was hard for him to swallow.

Malik was not treated the same as white people in the marines. He ended up being discharged. After the war Malik believed that the best way to achieve things was with violence. He joined the blank panthers and adopted much the same view that he had in Vietnam. Now the enemy was police and whites. Fortunately he realized that this was not the way to accomplish anything and reveals that they were "in the end just showing off."

Malik faced many adverse situations in his life. Most of these were out of his control. He however does not adopt a confrontational tone.. There is not a sense of remorse; he is more matter of fact. Or at least this is how the writer of Malik's story tells it. It lends itself to be very believable, and I sympathize with Malik.

Both bell hooks and Wallace Terry are writing about very different subjects but both arguments are made using personal stories. These real life actions of real life events gave the arguments validity. They function in a way in which you never doubt the author. How can you argue with something that happened to someone. It is much stronger and better reading personal experience as an argument than merely as a opinion paper, no matter how well written.

Student Sample Three:

Meta-Sequence Four: Private Experience as Public Argument
"Killing Rage"
"Ruth's Song"
"The Brass Ring and the Deep Blue Sea"
"On Being a Self Forever"; from *My Brother*
"Violet De Cristoforo--Tule Lake"
"Private First Class Reginald 'Malik'
Edwards, Phoenix, Louisiana"

Writing Prompt #1: Choose two to four readings from the above list. Write an analysis of the argument being made in each essay. In other words, what is the argument? How and what evidence is the writer using? How does this argument work? And so on. Include clear discussions about the part that private experience is playing within the arguments.

Senseless Violence or Valuable Trainer:
Paintball Pros and Cons

The two essays: "Private First Class Reginald 'Malik' Edwards, Phoenix, Arizona" and "Paintball as a Combat Sport" both deal with the same basic topic. This topic is, however, deeper than the first theory that most get upon initial reading; that they are about warfare, including the pros and cons of, to be blunt, "going through the motions" of acting out warfare. At one time, warfare was more than just a tool for killing the opposition: It was a sacred tool, with almost ritualistic rites that both performed, to regain whatever honor had been While this may seem arrogant, it is a better reason than today's view: "I don't like you, so I will kill you." The real topic is deeper than that, going to the psychological effects of real warfare, and the possible connection with play warfare. One other main point cold be claimed that paintball helps to show how fruitless actual warfare is. I prefer to combine these two theories into one: paintball, as a sport, can show one how quickly they can die in real combat, giving them a taste of what was experienced in real warfare, and thus forces them to think twice before wishing to go to war.

These two essays work together in a non-direct way. "Private" for example, shows the unethical side of warfare, with many examples of senseless bloodshed. "Paintball", on the other hand, discusses a fun sport that patronizes killing, yet also gives an example of what real combat would be like. Its saving grace is that each player that dies would return not much later, ready for another round. "Private" starts off with the harsh reality of warfare in the opening statements:

> "Not only did we receive one round, but three marines got wounded right off. Not only that, but one of the Marines was our

favorite Marine, Sergeant Bradford. This brother that everybody loved got shot in the groin." (201c)

Two paragraphs later he discusses grenading a hut full of children . . . not exactly the ethical way of performing warfare. It used to be that a soldier would first question identity of the unknown, and then shoot if required. In Vietnam, this had degraded to shooting first, and forget asking questions if they were still alive. If they were, then you shot again. Warfare had degraded to this, its lowest form. The pinnacle of warfare was during the Napoleonic War until the Revolutionary War. Originally, warfare was equal to a duel, except at a grander scale. This honor, however, could be the cause of senseless battles, such as one King insulting another by saying that "His hunting hounds stink. What? Men just died over a pack of dogs?" (Song of Albion, pg. 64) Up to this point, honor was more important than whoever was left standing at the end. Each army would march onto the field, dressed as best possible, and first tried to intimidate the other. If this failed, then the two would march at each other until hand to hand combat ensued. Those that were scared and broke rank were shot by their own troops to keep honor. However, this battle described in "Private" is furthest from this archetype. Here the main example of warfare was; "The mother-----hit, you call in some air. Bring in some heavy artillery, whatever you need to cool them down. You wipe that area up. You soften it up. Then you lay to see if you receive any fire. An then you go on in." (201 h) It had restored to the same style of warfare as in paintball, ditching for cover, let someone else set up cover fire, and then try to sneak in if all seems clear.

However, in paintball, one could reason that this realism in comparison to actual warfare is a good thing. So many times we are blasted with the myth that war is about one man walking up to 600 enemies, and killing them with their own weapons, all before dinner. In paintball, ones life is on the line, and hiding is part of the game. Those that try the initial flag cap are always the first to die, unless they are playing against the Helen Keller Clan. Another pro argument is now effective paintball can be when played to the utmost realism. This is done when both teams play in a set field, with mock buildings and bases, use red paint, and the dead lie where

88

they fall. When this type of round is played, as the author Jason Rein stated the following upon witnessing this event; "I must admit that it was a highly unusual sight to see individual 'bodies' (and in some cases clusters) as I made my way off the field." (pg. 154n) Due to this statement, he was one of the few lucky enough to survive. What he doesn't say numerically is how many of his teammates walked off when he did, but due to the wording in the statement, I doubt that many did. Most of his comrades were left on the field of play.

However, no matter how realistic paintball gets, it is still no match for the real thing. This is due to being able to watch the dead get up and wash the paint from their bodies. In real war, not only do they stay dead, but they also don't stay whole. On pg. 201g of "Private", the author describes one instant when he emptied a clip into a man running at him. The man was still alive, partially due to some of the rounds shooting through most of one of his arms, which later fell off as he dragged his 'kill' back to base as proof. The real problem with paintball is that it does not produce the fear one feels while in real combat. Certainly, one does not want to be shot. This is due more to wanting just to get a kill before feeling that trademark sting. The true fear of wanting to live, and fully realizing how close death is can only be experienced in real combat. This is best shown in the same description of shooting the man.

> Everybody was comin' congradulatin' me, saying what a great thing it was. I'm trying to be cool, but I'm really freakin' out. So then I start walking away, and they told me I had to carry the body back to base camp. All of a sudden is wasn't like I was carrying a gook. I was actually carrying a human being. I started feeling guilty. I just started feeling really badly. (201g, h)

It is this sense of humanity that cannot be fully realized in paintball. One sees the dead, especially when looking through a target scope, but unlike in real combat, the target would not drop. Instead, the 'dead' would shake their fist in the direction of the shooter, or swear, sometimes commenting on their own stupidity. In real combat, the shower of blood that proved a hit, was silently celebrated, amidst a panicked duck back in the brush,

89

along with silent prayers that the slain comrades had not seen where the killing shot had come from. This guerilla sniping was like poking a hornet's nest. Kill one or two, and the shooter may be secure in that position, as long as they were not spotted. Kill more than this, and the enemy would become brave enough in their anger to hunt down the shooter. Due to this, a trigger happy shooter would have to move often to keep from being killed himself, but each move made him vulnerable. The fewer times one had to move, the less chance there was of them being spotted.

This major difference between reality and make believe is the final dividing factor between the two. Paintball will never be able to completely replicate full out warfare, but this a good thing. One can see the sublime horror in paintball, and realize that warfare is many times worse than this. For one to claim that paintball is as evil as real warfare is like claiming that driving simulators are as real as the actual car. . .this is not the case, however. The controls may be realistic, but one could never feel the wind in the hair, or experience the thrill of having an open highway with no one around to slow you down. Paintball in itself is just a game, and will never have the same effect on people as actual warfare would. It does, however, give a prelude to what war is like, giving one the thrill of the kill, the 'soldiers high', while at the same time showing one the reality of the speed of death in actual combat. In this way, it acts as a deterrent, and hopefully, will someday save the lives of those that are 'killed' by red or green paint.

Student Sample Four:

Meta-Sequence Four: Private Experience as Public Argument
"Killing Rage"
"Ruth's Song"
'The Brass Ring and the Deep Blue Sea"
"On Being a Self Forever"
from *My Brother*
"Violet DeCristoforo--Tule Lake"
"Private First Class Reginald 'Malik" Edwards, Phoenix, Louisiana"

Writing Prompt #2: Write an essay about an important private experience of your own. Be sure to make use of both reflection and reflexivity. Beyond that, make sure that your essay is more than "just a story." In other words, make sure that you are fashioning a public argument from your own experiences. For help and ideas, return to your notes and ideas generated in your groups regarding how these other writers have made arguments based on their private experiences.

The Dead Self

All personal experiences involve a certain amount of self disclosure; however by talking about this experience I fear people will think different of me. It is very hard to explain something I am not proud of; but this compelling force has pulled me to get this skeleton out of my closet for years. As John Updike suggests, there are things stored in our pasts that are troublesome: "Such embedded data compose my most intimate self. . .beneath my more or less acceptable social,. . .performance" Uupdike 216). Keep in mind, I am no longer this person. John Updike says "not only are selves conditional but they die. Each day, we wake slightly altered, and the person we were yesterday is dead. . . It is even possible to dislike our old selves" (Updike 221). This is the self that I dislike, and the self that is dead. To parallel Updike thoughts with my story gave me comfort. At times we do have different selves, but that does not necessarily mean that the bad self is who we really are.

There it was, a beautiful black jacket I knew I had to have. It was simple, but classic; a must have for any outfit. Those were the superficial thoughts going through my mind the day I walked into the department store, without any money. Updike tells us [his] "awareness of an object is the object itself (the jacket in my case), the thing known and perceived without any person knowing and perceiving it" (Updike 219). As if I was the lion and the coat was the gladiator, the jacket was my pursuant. Who would suspect an innocent, carefree teenager, dressed well, seeming as though they had money to burn, which obviously was not the case. Initially, I knew it was not mine to have, just like a lot of things at any

91

given mall. But that day was different. I was with my best friend Natalie who recently became this master thief. I don't know if she had been hanging out with someone new, but all of a sudden she was a completely different person. She lived for gong to the mall- without any money. It wasn't just about having cute clothes to her, it was having name brands and new styles. I confessed my love of the jacket to her, and she said, "take it", so nonchalant, that she honestly felt that there was nothing wrong with it. It obviously didn't bother her that her father was a cop! I have been raised in the Catholic faith all my life, but for that hour, I didn't even know who I was. Updike explains moments like this in the following way. "These random bytes of recollection are part of my self, . . . blurred recollections, keeps me company during insomnia, and has an intelligence so feeble it sometimes forgets the Lord's Prayer" (Updike 213). I, too, have this memory and it keeps me company even though I might not want it to. It is my mind that reenacts my every move that day in my dreams, or are they haunting nightmares? This recollection has troubled me for years; however, at that moment, like Updike, I didn't know who God was, all that mattered was I needed that coat.

The first time I ever stole something was in sixth grade. I was at the mall with another friend of mine. I lifted a bottle of nail polish. The girl I was with praised me as if it was an act of kindness. She felt it was such a triumph; over who I have no idea. I became very quiet the rest of the day, and engrossed in an uncanny sickness. The kind where a big lump sits in your throat, and your stomach churns as if there is a butter mill in there. Before I left the mall I had to return the polish. It made me so sick to my stomach, I almost puked because I had taken it. I guess at the time I just wasn't strong enough. Or maybe it was that I was actually stronger. My friend said it was ok, and I naively trusted her. I look back now at my childhood and can vividly see the power of peer pressure.

I took the black jacket to the dressing room. For hours that seemed like minutes, I just admired myself. I looked beautiful, but only with the jacket. I sat alone in the dressing room. I stared at the back of a dressing room door, dazing in and out of consciousness. Then I turned to the mirror. I didn't see myself. I saw my parents. How scary was that? In a weird sense, my life was flashing before my eyes, everything I had ever learned about right and wrong, even the law itself; and I was actually going to take this jacket. My mind was spinning as I thought of all my options. But every time I could only come to one conclusion. Sure I can take it, it is over priced anyway. I know a lot of people that steal things everyday. The store isn't going to miss one jacket.

As I continued to rationalize stealing this jacket, the more I thought about it, the better it sounded. I wasn't doing anything wrong. I proceeded to put my arms through the sleeves. The soft, new cotton glided against my arm, giving me goose bumps, because it would soon be mine. The dressing room attendant knocked on the door as I was putting my jacket over the new one. My heart dropped. I fell to my ledge and my knees gave out in weakness. "Is everything ok in there?" "Just fine!," I replied. I couldn't think about it any longer. Quickly, I ripped off the tags and secured the black jacket under my own. I stayed along the outer edge of the store as I made my way to the door, waiting for Natalie outside. My breath was quick and my heart was beating so hard. I broke out in a cold sweat, never feeling so sick before in my life.

"Wasn't that easy?" Natalie asked, as if nothing had happened. I was a criminal! What was I going to tell my mom? That was the real judgement day. Of course that was my biggest concern at the age of 16. If I got passed her everything was smooth sailing. In fact I ran so quickly to my room, she didn't even see me. I sat on my bed and thanked God it was over. Thinking now, thanking God was a demented and ironic thing to do. The one person who knows my every moment probably looked down on me in disgust. But Updike says, "God, He is, a bottomless encouragement to our faltering and frightened being" (Updike 229). I know God would never turn His back on me, as I have done to Him time and again; but this time He knows I am truly sorry for His commandment that I have broken. However, to this day my mom doesn't know I stole that jacket, and I could never tell her. Through this ordeal, my greatest accomplishment was admitting it to myself. I knew it was something that had to be done, but this paper opened up the window of opportunity. This was my written confessional for myself. As badly as I feel, the more people I talk to, the more that have told me they have stolen too. Not that is excused my behavior, but I do take comfort in Updike's words: "that we age and leave behind this litter of dead, unrecoverable selves is both unbearable and the commonest thing in the world—it happens to everybody" (Updike 226). Stealing may not have been done by everybody, but I am sure everyone has done something that they are not necessarily proud of. With age we learn from our mistakes. The dead self is left to return to the dust it came from.

At the age of 16 I felt I was really mature, what a joke. But I can see the error of my ways. Growing up is so confusing when you feel pulled in so many directions. I could never make an excuse or justify my actions, just learn from my mistake. When I'm at the mall today I look at high school kids in disgust, assuming they have stolen something at least once in their lives, just because they have a large purse or a heavy coat. It is not to say that none of them have, but I'm sure my mom never thought I had stolen something either. But there are a lot of people out there that are a lot better than me. I know who I am now, and that person then wasn't me. I also know that I cannot form an opinion of someone on one wrongful, or insinuating act. God gave us free will to choose our actions, and temptation surrounds everyone everyday. "Our self is thrust into a manifold reality that is thoroughly gratuitous, and the faith in an afterlife, however much our reason ridicules it, very modestly extends out faith that each moment of our consciousness will be followed by another-that a coherent matrix has been prepared for this precious self of ours" (Updike 217). I believe everyone has a path in life. I stepped off track; nevertheless, more obstacles will come my way, I just need to have a little faith. Now it all seems like a surreal experience, finally laid to rest. Like Updike, my yesterday's self is dead (the self that stole the jacket), but also like Updike, my yesterday's self lives in memory, encompassing "my most intimate self."

Student Sample Five:

Chapter Two End-of-Chapter Sequences
Sequence Two: Self vs. Role
"Ruth's Song"
"The Hurt, Betrayed Son"
"An American of Color"

Writing Prompt #2:
Why do we have socially defined roles, anyway? What good are they?
Why can't we just "be ourselves"? Write an essay in which you attempt to
answer these questions, drawing evidence from the story of Ruth Steinem,
Rambo, or Victor Villanueva (or any combination of the three).

My Little Brother Melissa

When my sister Melissa was born my family consisted of her, my mother,
my father, my twin brother and myself. My brother Matt and I were about
three years old when she was born. My mother was excited to have
another female in the family for her to relate to. I on the other hand, told
everyone that I had a new brother. That is how Matt and I treated her.
Being submersed into a family full of guys was bound to rub off on her
and it did. No matter how hard my mother tried to make Melissa a little
girl she would not act like one. She was just another one of the guys.

Our gender does not come from our biology, but it is formed by the
culture in which we are brought up. I believe that people are programmed
from the day that they are born to act a certain way based on their gender.
I think that if it was possible to completely reverse what society thinks
male and female roles should be than the genders would actually switch.
This would mean that everything would have to be reversed. The mother-
daughter relationships and father-son relationships would have to be
reversed, the culture's views on each gender's emotional characteristics
would have to be reversed, all of the advertisements that are gender
directed would have to be switched, and everything else that separates
gender except biology. If all of this is changed than I think that it is

possible to have the female gender in a male body or vise versa. My sister is an example of someone who I think was partially programmed to associate herself with the male gender. Of course she was not totally submersed into a society where genders are reversed.

The example above, is just a small one. Even though she acted like a guy and dressed like a guy she did not have all of the characteristics of the male gender. There were too many outside sources showing her what a little girl should act like. She was influenced by everything from friends at school to television advertisements.

Though my sister acted in many ways like a male, she also had some characteristics of a female. One of these female characteristics she exhibited is shown in the toys that she played with. She played with some of the same toys that my brother and I enjoyed like Lincoln Logs and Matchbox cars but she also played with some toys like her "My Little Pony" dolls and a few "Barbie" dolls. The main reason for her interest in the dolls and other girl toys is the advertising done by the companies. The television advertisements for the dolls showed little girls having a grand old time with their dolls while the ads for the boy toys showed a group of guys have fun with their toys. I am sure that this had an influence as to what toys my sister wanted to buy when our mother took us to the toy store. In the store there is just as much gender targeted advertisement as on television. The store is pretty much divided in half between the boy toys and the girl toys. I know that you can tell when you are in the girl toy section of the toy store. Just look at the colors. They are filled with pink and purple. When Melissa would find a toy she saw in an advertisement, she would find herself surrounded by isles and isles of other girl toys influencing her more as to which toys she should like to play with. If she was constantly exposed to the television commercials showing little girls playing with toy cars I am sure that she would be influenced to go buy toy cars. On the same note, if the girl and boy sections of the toy store were reversed than the gender roles could easily be reversed.

Melissa's actions were also similar to that of a member of the male gender. It is not uncommon for her to get into a wrestling match with my father in the living room. She enjoyed watching WWF wrestling so much that she would buy tickets to go see it in person when it came to town. She is also know to just throw a friendly punch into someone's arm like a male would. She seems to have that violent characteristic that males have been branded with. My mother got Melissa into taking piano lessons. My mother's plans to keep a little bit of the female gender in her little girl backfired when my sister started high school. She joined a Rock band with four other guys. I know that there are numerous female singers but for a female keyboardist to be a musician in the background of a male band is fairly uncommon. My mother was not very pleased that Melissa wanted to play in a band but mom knew that it was that Melissa wanted to do. She was in and out of a couple of different bands in high school. I do not think that she would have been so interested in playing in a band if she did not have the influence of so many males growing up.

Another way gender is programmed into the minds of our culture is through emotion. I can once again use the example of my sister. As long as I can remember, she has never been a very emotional girl. She grew up with the guys in the family who did not show very much emotion. I think that this influenced how she shows her emotion. She handles emotional situations very similar to the way that my brother, my father, and I do. My mother handles them in a completely different way than the four of us do. When Melissa is upset she does not cry. She may be a little quiet or she may seem a little bit distant, but she does not let her feelings known. This is how the guys in our family show emotion. She is a freshman at the University of Georgia now and she has become a little bit more emotional, but that is due to the fact that she shares a dorm suite with five other girls. She acts like all of the rest of the girls in the dorm do. She is still not as emotional as her roommates who grew up with other female influences but she is more like a female now than ever. I think that if she had more of a female influence growing up, she would have been a more emotional girl.

I think that the male influence she was exposed to growing up effected whom she chose to associate herself with. When Melissa was growing up she always seemed to have more guy friends than she did girl friends. You would think that a mother would worry a lot about this situation, but my mother did not. She realized that Melissa just did not like how all the girls in her school acted. As she was known to put it, "There are way too many stupid, emotional girls in my school." She got along better with guys than she did with girls. Even until she graduated from high school I only remember a couple of girls ever hanging out with Melissa at our house. I think that she found it easier to relate to the mentality of her male peers than that of her female peers. I think that to her guy friends she was just considered one of the guys as well. I think that if she had more of a female influence growing up, she would have found it easier to relate to her female peers and they may have found it easier to relate to her.

I think that Doug Robinson's essay describes Melissa's situation best. Robinson argued that gender is programmed into our brains. He said that it is programmed by culture and the influence of others while an individual is growing up. I think that Melissa only went through a small amount of influence towards the male gender in comparison to all of the influences outside of the family. I think that if she was as similar to a male as she was with only my family influencing her, than if everything would influence girls to display the male gender from birth than I think it is possible for the male and female gender roles to switch.